PRAISE FOR *FREQUENCY*

"Robert Morris makes an important truth very clear: we cannot consistently and reliably recognize God's voice if we are strangers to His Word. As our loving Father, God desires a relationship with His children. He revealed Himself in His Word, not so we could have a personal fellowship with a book but with a living, all-knowing, love-filled Father.

"The spirit realm is filled with sounds. Many are subtle, distracting, deceiving impressions. It is imperative that believers know God's Word to discern these sounds. Robert helps you reach that place where, as one of God's sheep, you will be able to hear and recognize the Shepherd's voice. You will begin experiencing a relationship some people never imagined possible, but the God of the impossible makes it an ever-present reality."

—James Robison

Founder and president, Life Outreach International;

and founder and publisher, *The Stream* (stream.org)

"*Frequency* is a safe and sure guide for discerning and heeding God's voice as God's Word teaches us this discipline. Robert Morris provides insight for learning to live 'in tune' with God's heart: a pathway that forms character, begets a genuine humility, and brings godly growth in an obedient, sensitive, and sensible lifestyle of intimacy with our Creator."

—Jack W. Hayford

Pastor emeritus, The Church On The Way

"From reading the Bible we know God spoke to people audibly as well as through prophets, dreams, visions, and circumstances. While we can always trust what God says to us through His Word, it can be tricky to know when God is speaking in other ways. That's why I'm so excited about Pastor Robert Morris's new book, *Frequency: Tune In. Hear God.* In this important book he clearly shows different ways in which God still speaks today and helps us learn how to recognize when God is speaking. If we're listening, God is speaking."

—Craig Groeschel

Senior pastor, LifeChurch.tv; and author,

From This Day Forward

"Let *Frequency* and Robert Morris be your spiritual trainer as you learn to hear God's voice and watch your life and faith soar to a new level. You won't regret it."

—John Maxwell

#1 *New York Times* bestselling author

"Robert Morris has been a close, personal friend of mine for more than twenty years. He is truly a man who hears from God. The secret to his success is very simple: he seeks God, he hears God, and he obeys God. This book will help you do the same. I highly recommend it to anyone wanting to grow in his relationship with the Lord and experience greater victory in life."

—Jimmy Evans

Founder and CEO, MarriageToday

"I've known Robert Morris for many years, and I've always been amazed at his ability to hear God speak in a clear and authoritative way. In *Frequency* Robert shares his experiences—good and bad—and gives readers some practical tools for tuning in to the one voice they need to hear more than any other."

—Dave Ramsey

New York Times bestselling author and nationally syndicated radio show host

"'How can I hear God?' asks both the believer and skeptic and is the question Pastor Robert Morris is asked most often. It is an oft-repeated question I hear as I travel. Hearing God begins with a relationship with Him, 'an awesome privilege' and 'an awesome responsibility' that involves being 'careful stewards of God's voice,' writes Morris. In these pages you will hear from one with a tender heart for God, a lifetime of wrestling with these issues and a longing to connect people to Him. I am delighted to endorse my friend Robert Morris's book and know his words will encourage, teach, and inspire you."

—Ravi Zacharias

Author and speaker

"One of my favorite things about the Lord is that we can hear His voice. In *Frequency* Pastor Robert has given many great tools on the value of God's voice and how to listen and seek what He is saying through the different ways He communicates with His children. This book will draw you closer to the Father's heart as you find out how relational He is and learn about His longing to personally communicate with you right in the midst of your everyday life."

—Kari Jobe Carnes

Dove Award–winning and Grammy-nominated recording artist

"Our lives are often filled with static, making it hard to hear the most important messages God is trying to get to us. That's why I'm excited that my friend Robert Morris has written *Frequency*. Tuning into God's voice is a spiritual skill that Robert has developed through years of faithful leadership and ministry. Let him be your audiologist as this book tests your ability to hear from God and develop your skill to hear God's message for your life."

—Steven Furtick

Elevation Church founder and *New York Times* bestselling author, *Crash the Chatterbox* and *Sun Stand Still*

"The best advice I could ever give anyone is, 'Listen to Jesus, and do what He says.' But as believers we don't always understand *how* to hear from God or *when* it's Him speaking to us. That's why I love Robert Morris's new book, *Frequency*. Robert so clearly and eloquently breaks down the many ways God speaks to His people. I promise you that reading the pages of this book will draw you closer to Jesus as you learn to hear His voice more clearly."

—Perry Noble

Senior pastor, NewSpring Church

FREQUENCY

FREQUENCY

TUNE IN. HEAR GOD.

ROBERT MORRIS

W PUBLISHING GROUP

AN IMPRINT OF THOMAS NELSON

Published in Nashville, Tennessee, by W Publishing Group, an imprint of Thomas Nelson.

Published in association with the literary agency of Winters & King, Inc.

Thomas Nelson titles may be purchased in bulk for educational, business, fund-raising, or sales promotional use. For information, please e-mail SpecialMarkets@ThomasNelson.com.

Unless otherwise noted, Scripture quotations are taken from the New King James Version®. © 1982 by Thomas Nelson. Used by permission. All rights reserved.

Scripture quotations marked NIV are taken from the Holy Bible, New International Version®, NIV®. © 1973, 1978, 1984, 2011 by Biblica, Inc.® Used by permission of Zondervan. All rights reserved worldwide.

Scripture quotations marked NLT are taken from *Holy Bible*, New Living Translation. © 1996, 2004, 2007, 2013 by Tyndale House Foundation. Used by permission of Tyndale House Publishers, Inc., Carol Stream, Illinois 60188. All rights reserved.

Scripture quotations marked GNT are taken from the Good News Translation in Today's English Version—Second Edition. © 1992 by American Bible Society. Used by permission.

Scripture quotation taken from the New American Standard Bible®. © 1960, 1962, 1963, 1968, 1971, 1972, 1973, 1975, 1977, 1995 by The Lockman Foundation. Used by permission.

Scripture quotation taken from *The Message*. © by Eugene H. Peterson 1993, 1994, 1995, 1996, 2000, 2001, 2002. Used by permission of Tyndale House Publishers, Inc.

Scripture quotations marked ESV are taken from the ESV® Bible (The Holy Bible, English Standard Version®). © 2001 by Crossway, a publishing ministry of Good News Publishers. Used by permission. All rights reserved.

Scripture quotations marked CEV are taken from the Contemporary English Version. © 1991, 1992, 1995 by American Bible Society. Used by permission.

Italics added to Scripture quotations are the author's own emphasis.

ISBN 978-0-7180-8109-6 (IE)

Library of Congress Cataloging-in-Publication Data

Names: Morris, Robert (Robert Preston), 1961–
Title: Frequency : tune in, hear God / Robert Morris.
Description: Nashville : W Publishing Group, an imprint of Thomas Nelson, 2016. |
    Includes bibliographical references.
Identifiers: LCCN 2015031934 | ISBN 9780718011116
Subjects: LCSH: Spirituality—Christianity. | Listening—Religious
    aspects—Christianity.
Classification: LCC BV4501.3 .M67378 2016 | DDC 248—dc23 LC record available at
    http://lccn.loc.gov/2015031934

Printed in the United States of America

17 18 19 20 RRD 6

This book is dedicated to the members of Gateway Church. They have the most fervent desire that I have ever seen to hear God's voice and walk with Him.

It is the nature of God to speak.

—A. W. Tozer

CONTENTS

HOW CAN I HEAR GOD?

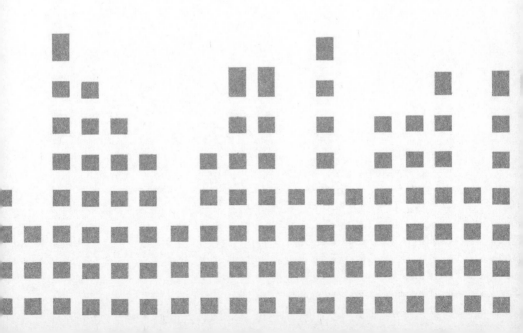

He who is of God hears God's words.

—John 8:47

The bush caught fire but never turned to ash.

It just kept burning, burning, burning without being consumed, and the shepherd was so intrigued by the strange sight that he left the flock of sheep he was tending to come closer to the blazing foliage.

Nothing like this had ever happened before on the far side of the wilderness near the mountain of Horeb, at least nothing that the shepherd had ever seen before. Nothing around the bush was burning—just the one bush. As the shepherd peered intently at the strange sight, the flames continued to lick the branches, dance around the bush's leaves, and emit heat and smoke like any old normal fire would do, but the shepherd knew now that this was no normal fire.

The day was about to turn even stranger, although the shepherd didn't know it just yet. The Lord saw that the man had gone over to look, so a Voice called to the man from within the bush: "Moses! Moses!"

You might think if a man heard a voice coming from an unusual place such as a burning bush that he'd turn on his heel and sprint for the hills. Or maybe he'd take his staff and give the bush a good whack, thinking he'd gone crazy and was hearing things. These were the days long before microphones and speakers. If a voice was heard, it was only heard from a person. How could a person be within the fire that burned a bush?

But the shepherd didn't run. The shepherd responded to the Voice by saying simply, "Here I am" (Ex. 3:4). He must have sensed something familiar in the sound of the Voice—something that was both incredibly strong and incredibly comforting at the same time.

"Do not come any closer," said the Voice from out of the bush. "Take off your sandals, for the place where you are standing is holy ground. . . .

I am the God of your father, the God of Abraham, the God of Isaac and the God of Jacob" (vv. 5–6 NIV).

And the strange and wonderful conversation continued from there.

Hearing the Voice of God

Whenever I hear this phrase, "Pastor Robert, can I ask you something?" I have a good hunch what's coming.

It's because in more than thirty years of ministry, I've heard the same great question posed time and time again. This question is from people in my own congregation, students in university classes I've taught, people who seek my counsel when I'm the guest speaker at other churches, and pastors and leaders at conferences.

The question is, "How can I hear God?"

Sometimes the question is phrased slightly differently: "How can I learn to hear God's voice more clearly?" or "How can I discern God's voice?" or "How can I tell that God is speaking to me?" But the heart behind the question is the same. People aren't looking for burning bushes exactly. But just like Moses, they want to be available if and when God speaks to them. They want to connect with God on a deeper level and understand how to hear the voice of God.

I'm writing this book to provide a more fully developed answer to this question. A fuller, broader answer is needed because the explanation as to how to hear God's voice can't be given in a quick formula. Rather, it arises intrinsically as part of a genuine and ongoing relationship with God. If you want to hear God's voice, then you must get to know God as a person—and this takes time and intention, much the same as it takes to know any friend.

As A. W. Tozer said,

I believe that much of our religious unbelief is due to a wrong conception of and a wrong feeling for the Scriptures of Truth. A silent God suddenly began to speak in a book and when the book was finished lapsed back into silence again forever. Now we read the book as the record of what God said when He was for a brief time in a speaking mood.

With notions like that in our heads how can we believe?

The facts are that God is not silent, has never been silent. It is the nature of God to speak. The second Person of the Holy Trinity is called the *Word*. The Bible is the inevitable outcome of God's continuous speech. It is the infallible declaration of His mind for us put into our familiar human words.

I think a new world will arise out of the religious mists when we approach our Bible with the idea that it is not only a book which was once spoken, but a book which is *now speaking*.[1]

Rest assured, God has always been a speaking God, and God still speaks to us today. Fifteen times in the New Testament alone, Jesus says, "He who has ears, let him hear." In John 8:47, Jesus says, "He who is of God hears God's words." And in John 10:27, Jesus says, "My sheep hear My voice, and I know them, and they follow Me." Read those verses again if you need to. Note the key conversation words in each verse just mentioned: *hear*, *God's words*, and *voice*.

Certain Christian leaders insist that God has stopped speaking today or that God speaks only through the pages of Scripture—and if you can't name a book, chapter, and verse, then God hasn't spoken. Largely, they base this thinking on Revelation 22:18–19, where God warns people not to add anything to Scripture.

I strongly hold to the teaching of Revelation 22:18–19, the same way I hold to all the Bible's teaching. God warns us not to add anything to Scripture, and I agree. We can't add to Scripture. We must not add to Scripture. And yet Scripture indicates that God still speaks. So we must reconcile these two truths.

Perhaps the very terminology *God speaks* creates the tension in the first place. So we need to define what we're talking about. There's the work of God that we call *inspiration*—where God guided men to write Scripture, with the result the same as if God had written it. And then there's the *prompting of the Holy Spirit* for conviction, guidance, assurance, and wisdom. Both of these works of God are classified under the overall umbrella of *God speaks*, but these works are not the same. When the Holy Spirit led me to start Gateway Church, where I'm senior pastor today, I very much heard God speak to my heart about the matter. Yet just because I heard God speak, that doesn't mean I could write down what the Holy Spirit impressed upon me and insist that I had another book of the Bible.

So there are two truths to reconcile: (1) Scripture is finished. Yes. (2) And the Holy Spirit still guides and prompts and convicts and leads. Yes. It's this second concept that I refer to in this book when I say, "God speaks." God speaks to us in our spirits. His Spirit bears witness with our spirit. God does not give us additional books of the Bible. He doesn't speak to us audibly. We don't hear His voice the same way we would hear someone on the telephone.

Yet He still speaks.

God Speaks to Your Heart

Years ago my former pastor, Olen Griffing, got in trouble from the leaders of his denomination because he believed and preached that God still speaks today. The leaders formed a credentialing committee, met, and questioned Pastor Olen for several hours about the matter. Finally Pastor Olen addressed the committee chairman, a pastor, and said, "You've been asking me questions for three hours. Please let me ask you something now."

The man nodded, and so Olen asked him, "Were you called to preach?"

The man nodded again, and so Olen added, "Who called you to preach?"

The man cleared his throat and said, "Well, God did."

Olen said, "Good. Would you mind telling me which verse in the Bible contains your name and says that you were called to preach?"

The man put his head down and said nothing.

Pastor Olen summed it up: "God never says anything to our hearts that's contrary to what is already revealed in the Bible. But in the same way He called you to preach, He continues to speak to people's hearts everywhere. That's how God still speaks today."

Let me simply say that it's never my intent in this book to create dissension within the Christian community. In fact, I'd say most of us are on the same page already. We sometimes just use different terminology, like Olen did with his credentialing committee. The spirit of unity in the body of Christ is what I want to champion.

Both the Old and New Testaments clearly describe God as a speaking God. The real task—and wonderful opportunity—is for us to learn to hear His voice. That's what I want to turn our attention toward because that's my burden for all Christians everywhere. We need to know that God still speaks to His children today, and we need to know how to listen to Him and then respond accordingly. I want every believer to have an intimate, ongoing, and passionate relationship with Jesus Christ so that we will all love and serve and follow His voice.

Friends, the good news is that we don't need to go through life blindly. We don't need to rely on our own understanding. That truth that God still speaks today offers us hope and reassurance and confidence.

You can learn to hear God!

—ROBERT MORRIS
DALLAS, TEXAS

CHAPTER ONE

THE BEAUTY OF BEING SHEEP

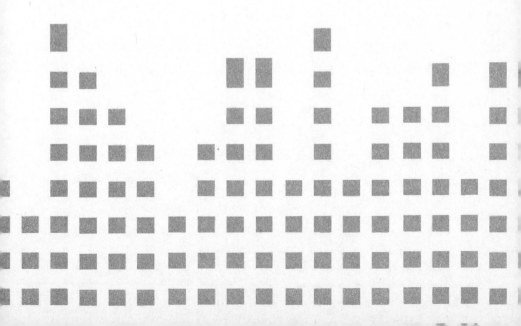

When he brings out his own sheep, he goes before them;
and the sheep follow him, for they know his voice.

—John 10:4

Say you're in a small group at your church and want to break the ice, so you play a little game to start things off. A great game for this purpose is called Two Truths and a Lie—have you ever played it? You make three statements about yourself, the more outrageous the better. Two of the statements will be true, and one statement will be false. Then the other people in the room try to guess which statement isn't true about you.

So let's play that game, right here, right now. I'll start by telling you a story that includes three statements about myself. Two will be true, and one won't. You guess the lie. Here it goes:

- **Statement one**: My wife, Debbie, and I have been married for more than thirty-five years. Can you imagine that? Thirty-five years!
- **Statement two**: During that time we've been through highs and lows, joy and sorrow, children and grandchildren, and everything in between. I'd say that after thirty-five years together, Debbie knows me pretty well, and I know Debbie pretty well too.
- **Statement three** (this is actually more than a statement; it's a little story in itself): Just last week, Debbie called me on the phone and greeted me with one word, "Hey."

  And I said, "Who is this?"

  And she said, "Uh . . . it's your wife, Debbie."

  And I said, "Debbie who?"

  And she said, "You know . . . Debbie. Debbie Morris. Your wife. We've been married for more than thirty-five years. You remember me, don't you?"

  End of story.

Okay, what are the two truths, and what's the lie?

The part about Debbie and I being married for more than thirty-five years is true.

And the part about us being through highs and lows and everything in between is true.

But the part about me not recognizing Debbie's voice on the phone is false. I'm sure you got that. Do you know why it's false? Because after more than thirty-five years together I can easily recognize her voice. Her voice is instantly familiar to me. I don't even need to ask who it is. All Debbie needs to say is one word on the end of a phone—*hey*—and there's no doubt in my mind it's my wife.

What's my point?

Jesus calls us to a similarly close relationship with Him where we instantly recognize His voice. And it doesn't take thirty-five years either. Can you imagine how great this is? The God of the universe invites us to enjoy a familiar relationship with Him, a relationship where we pray to Him, and He listens to us, and where He speaks and we listen to Him. A true dialogue.

There's a foundational truth that we need to grasp right up front, the glorious truth that God wants to talk to us in the first place. You need to grab hold of that amazing truth. If you don't, then you could dive into the Bible with a niggling doubt that there's anything to this experience of God speaking. Maybe God doesn't want to talk to you. Maybe He guards His counsel and never lets it out.

But no, God wants to talk to you and me. God even wants us to depend on hearing from Him as we depend on inhaling our next lungful of air to breathe. In Matthew 4:4, Jesus, when being tempted by the Devil, quotes Deuteronomy 8:3: "Man shall not live by bread alone, but by every word that proceeds from the mouth of God." Did you catch that? We're to live on the words that come out of God's mouth. They nourish and feed us, even better than real food does.

That truth can be staggering if you've never thought about it before. Because that is how God primarily wants us to live—not by our consciences, or by our pastor's teaching, or by our attendance at church each Sunday.

God wants us to live by His voice.

Living by God's Voice

Sometimes we Christians have a hard time living this way. We aren't familiar with the idea of living by the voice of God. It sounds weird, maybe even a little spooky. The people who go around saying that they hear from God get put in straitjackets, don't they?

But ask yourself this question: What's the main difference between a person who believes in Jesus Christ and a person who doesn't? Or let's make this personal: If you're a Christian, what's the main difference between you and an unbeliever?

It's that you have a personal relationship with God.

In a personal relationship, what you experience with God isn't merely religion. You don't just check a box beside a certain denomination, or mentally agree to a bunch of facts about God. Rather, you experience a deep and profound connection to God by His Son, Jesus Christ. Your relationship is personal because it's something you experience alone. Your grandfather can't have this faith for you. Your pastor can't make this connection for you. A personal relationship with God is what the apostle Paul describes in Ephesians 5:22–33. Jesus Christ is a living, thinking, acting person, and Paul describes by analogy how Jesus loves the church the same way a husband loves his wife.

So a personal relationship must involve communication—it must. Otherwise, how could a person ever have a personal relationship with God? If true dialogue doesn't take place, then it would be a one-sided attempt at communication, with us staring up into the sky, talking to God but hearing nothing in return.

God speaks. That's biblical fact. The pattern is established throughout Scripture that God communicates with humankind. God spoke to Adam and Eve in the garden of Eden. He spoke to Noah and to Abraham, Isaac, and Jacob. He spoke to Moses and to Isaiah, Jeremiah, Ezekiel, and Daniel—and to all the prophets. He spoke to men and women, to Deborah and Ruth. In the New Testament, He spoke to Mary, Peter, Paul, Jude, James, and John on the island of Patmos. In the time since then, God hasn't gotten laryngitis. He hasn't decided to change His nature and become mute. God still speaks—and this can give us great confidence in life.

A friend told me he was looking for a new job and had three strong leads. All three looked good, and he was trying to make a decision, so he asked me what he should do. We talked for some time, and I learned that he had done his homework, gathered facts, and carefully weighed the position, location, and salary of each job. Yet he was concerned about unknown factors. Maybe one of the companies would relocate in the future. Maybe the supervisor in one position would turn out to be a tyrant. Or perhaps a company was hiding its true financial picture and about to go bankrupt.

I said to him, "You just need to hear God."

That's one of the big differences between how a Christian makes a decision and how an unbeliever makes a decision. A Christian can hear the voice of God and discern God's will for his life. You can sense the direction God wants you to go. Wouldn't you rather make a decision about your life's future with the help of God's knowledge, rather than merely your own knowledge? We need to hear God's voice in so many areas of our lives—our jobs, our families, our friendships, our health, our areas of service, our futures. The only way we can walk in certainty is by hearing God. It's wrapped into our very identities as believers.

As a senior pastor, I absolutely need to hear from God. There's no way I can fulfill the responsibility of leading a church unless God is leading me. My intellect won't cut it. My seminary studies won't cut it. My talent or personality won't cut it. And I certainly don't have good looks to depend on. The only way I can lead a church is by having a daily, personal, intimate walk with God. I need to listen to God and hear God. He leads. I follow.

So let's take an in-depth look at John 10, one of the foundational Bible passages that describe this type of close relationship with God. John 10 underscores this truth for us: God wants us to live by hearing His voice.

We Are Sheep

Hearing God's voice is a question of identity. Who are you at your core?

The answer is this: you are a sheep.

We need to understand this important distinction right up front. Hearing God's voice is not about something we do. Rather, hearing God is about someone we are. Hearing God is not primarily a behavior. It's a reflection of our identity. We hear God because of who we are and because of whose we are.

In John 10, Jesus explains this idea in depth. Jesus calls Himself the Good Shepherd, and He contrasts the work He does with the work of Satan, a thief and a robber. Satan comes only to steal, kill, and destroy. But Jesus the Good Shepherd comes that people might have life, and have it abundantly (vv. 8, 10–11).

We are the sheep in the John 10 passage. How's that for a thought? Next time you meet a Christian friend, greet him by saying, "Hey, I'm a sheep, and guess what—so are you." If he gives you a look like you're completely loony then add, "I thought I smelled something funny."

The whole idea of our being sheep is that our identities are rooted in a shepherd-to-sheep model. Being a sheep is what a human being was designed to be. Sheep, by their very nature, need a guide. It's not that we hear God because of some action we take. Rather, we hear God because we were designed to hear God. Note John 10:1–5:

> Most assuredly, I say to you, he who does not enter the sheepfold by the door, but climbs up some other way, the same is a thief and a robber. But he who enters by the door is the shepherd of the sheep. To him the doorkeeper opens, and the sheep hear his voice; and he calls his own sheep by name and leads them out. And when he brings out his own sheep, he goes before them; and the sheep follow him, for they know his voice. Yet they will by no means follow a stranger, but will flee from him, for they do not know the voice of strangers.

Notice the sequence of events in this portion of Scripture. It's like a mini-movie playing out right before us. In the first scene, Jesus, the Shepherd of the sheep, enters the sheepfold directly, by way of the door. He doesn't sneak around and climb over the fence as a robber would do. Jesus, by way of His identity as the Good Shepherd, has familiar and direct access to the lives of His sheep.

In this second scene, when Jesus enters the sheepfold, Jesus speaks to the sheep, and the sheep hear His voice. He calls His own sheep by name, and He leads them out. He walks before them, and they follow Him. They wouldn't follow a stranger or a robber because they don't know the voice of a stranger or robber. But they follow Jesus. They know His voice.

Someone might ask: Are you sure that these sheep are actually a picture of us? Maybe John is talking about someone else. To answer that question, note John 10:16: "And other sheep I have which are not of this fold; them also I must bring, and they will hear My voice; and there will be one flock and one shepherd."

The overall context in John 10 is that Jesus is speaking to Jews, telling them that He's their Shepherd. He's their Messiah. If you're not Jewish, then the question of whether this passage applies to you is legitimate. But rest assured, it does apply to you. In John 10:16, Jesus tells the Jews that He has other sheep too—the Gentiles. That's the rest of us—people who aren't Jewish. These sheep, too, hear Jesus' voice, and both Jews and Gentiles ultimately come together in one flock. This is what Paul described in Galatians 3:28, when he said, "There is neither Jew nor Greek . . . for you are all one in Christ Jesus." So keep that teaching in mind, and then note John 10:27: "My sheep hear My voice, and I know them, and they follow Me."

So this one flock made up of both Jews and Gentiles, what does it do? We hear the voice of Jesus. He knows us, and we follow Him. We sheep hear the voice of Jesus, and Jesus leads us forward.

Where does Jesus lead us? Psalm 23 gives us a beautiful picture. Jesus leads us to green pastures, to areas of provision and rest. He leads us safely through dark valleys filled with troubles and uncertainties. He is always before us with His rod and staff of guidance and comfort. He prepares a bountiful feast of provision, even in the presence of our enemies, right in the very face of opposition. And ultimately, Jesus leads us to heaven, where we dwell in the house of the Lord forever. I love that imagery!

So the teaching in John 10 is clear. Who is Jesus? Jesus is our Good Shepherd. And what are we? We're sheep. And how does the Good Shepherd guide His sheep? By His voice. That's how we're to live: by listening to Jesus' voice. We're to depend on hearing His voice regularly and clearly.

Foundational Truths of Hearing God's Voice

Let's face it. Sometimes sheep don't listen to the Good Shepherd. The Bible shows example after example of people doing their own thing.

Sometimes people don't listen because of willful disobedience. At other times people don't listen because they haven't yet learned to hear God's voice. The good news is that we can learn to walk in this part of our identity. We can learn to hear God's voice.

So let's take a closer look at this part of our identity and see how we can cultivate this ability to hear God. My goal in this chapter is to make sure you know that hearing God's voice is something you were designed to do. God has given you the ability to communicate with Him spiritually. He wants to speak to you.

Three truths spring from the greater teaching surrounding John 10.

1. Our Ability to Hear God Is Innate

If something is *innate*, it is part of our instinct. Hearing God comes naturally to us as believers. Sheep are born as sheep. They're born with the innate ability to hear a shepherd. It's woven into the very sequence of their DNA. Lions don't have this ability. Rhinoceroses don't have this ability. Bumblebees don't have this ability. But sheep do. It's part of their instinct. The Bible calls us sheep, and the sheep instinct is true of us: when we become Christians, we are born with the ability to hear God's voice.

If we ever fear that we won't hear God's voice, we should take heart because God will speak to us. In John 10, He declares that He Himself is the Good Shepherd, and He promises that His sheep hear His voice. When we trusted Christ for our salvation, we were reborn with spiritual ears. When we were born again (John 3:7), and when we came alive in Christ (Eph. 2:4–6), we received this ability. It's part of our new nature, our new instinct, to be able to hear God. We became spiritual sheep, and spiritual sheep hear the Good Shepherd—Jesus. This is a great truth. It takes the worry out of the equation.

Debbie and I have traveled to Israel several times, and we've talked to native Israeli shepherds. One shepherd described to us how several flocks of sheep congregate together in one field, and one flock mixes in with another flock because the grazing is good in that particular location. The shepherds may be on the other side of the field, visiting as a bunch, chatting with other shepherds who've all brought their flocks to the same area that day. The shepherds talk, laugh, tell jokes, and then eventually it becomes time to go home at the end of the day. So one shepherd makes a small specific noise, maybe *ep*, and he starts walking. All of his sheep hear his voice, leave the rest of the sheep, and follow the shepherd they know. The next shepherd makes a different small, specific noise, maybe *ha*, and he starts walking. All of his sheep leave and follow him. And so on and so on until all the sheep are following the shepherd they're supposed to be with.

There are two categories in our discussion: (1) literal sheep and a literal shepherd, and (2) Christians and Jesus. A big difference between these two categories is that animals can't communicate intimate details of their lives to their shepherd, but Christians can communicate intimate details of their lives to God. Think of how fantastic that is.

Scientists are trying to figure out if animals use actual words, and certainly, animals can communicate to some degree with other animals and maybe even learn a word or two as a command. But listen to me: you don't need a PhD in zoology to know that animals don't use language the same way we do. If you have a dog, try this experiment at home. Call your dog over to you, pet his head and scratch around his ears, adopt a kind, sweet, syrupy voice, and say, "You're so stupid. Yes, you are. You're the most stupid dog I've ever met." He'll just wag his tail and grin as if you've given him the best compliment ever.

Animals don't use words. But humans do. We were born again with the ability to communicate and listen to specific thoughts with and from our God. We were born to talk with God. To hear His voice. To follow His leading. It's woven into our very DNA as spiritual sheep. We can innately hear God's voice.

2. Our Ability to Hear God Is Not Only Innate—It Is Learned

The question arises: If we're born with the innate ability to hear God, then why do we need to learn this ability too? Why is it necessary to be taught how to hear God, since the ability to hear spiritually is given to us as a gift upon our salvation?

It's a good question. The tension between our innate ability to hear God and our need to learn to hear Him is similar to the balance of the two truths that we innately know how to pray yet need to learn to pray. In Luke 11, the disciples of Jesus had been following Him everywhere. They had seen Him praying to God the Father on many occasions. They'd undoubtedly prayed with Him on various occasions. Yet the disciples still asked Jesus to teach them how to pray. And Jesus gave them a model to learn by, the one we popularly call the Lord's Prayer.

The same pattern holds true for us. If we're brand-new Christians, we can pray just by opening our mouths and talking to God. (And God hears us too. First John 5:14 says, "Now this is the confidence that we have in Him, that if we ask anything according to His will, He hears us.") Yet even though we can pray instantly as believers, we can also learn to pray as we grow in our faith. We learn to pray by studying the prayers of the Bible, by being taught how to pray by godly and more mature Christians, and by sheer practice in communication and development in our relationships with God. We pray, and we pray, and we pray, and we pray. And He speaks, and He speaks, and He speaks, and He speaks. And over time we gradually learn the ebbs and flows of the second half of prayer—listening to God. As we mature, we begin to understand that prayer is not about giving God a list of things for Him to do. Instead, God wants to have a relationship with us. This relationship is dynamic and personal. God has ears to listen, and He also has a mouth to speak. We have an innate ability to hear Him, but this ability is also learned.

Or think of it this way: children are born with the ability to communicate. But even then, they need to be taught how to speak and listen.

Think of all that's needed to learn how to speak. A baby starts off by learning simple, individual words—*mama, food, mine*. Then she needs to be taught how to string those words together and form sentences. After that, the sentences and communication become more complex. She needs to learn how to use grammar properly. She needs to learn how one word can be turned into a question simply by changing the inflection of her voice (*Who? What?*). She learns about synonyms, antonyms, and those tricky homonyms—words that are spelled and pronounced the same way but have different meanings (such as *row* a boat but put chairs in a *row*). Again, the baby's speech emerges because it's an innate ability of being human; yet it's also learned. You begin life with the ability to speak and understand speech programmed into you, yet you need to learn how to speak and listen too.

A friend of mine, Mike, played golf on the PGA Tour and was a professional for sixteen years. He's on our church staff now, but sometimes he and I will go out and golf together. A fantastic golf score is in the sixties, and even today, he rarely scores higher than a seventy. Me—well, let's just say when he and I go golfing, I'm in for a much, much longer game. It can be frustrating for me if I compare my golfing ability with his, but I need to remind myself that he was a professional. Think of all the time and practice he put in.

Similarly, when we're around mature Christians who have stories from their years of walking with God where He's clearly and sometimes miraculously spoken, we can feel down on ourselves. But God doesn't call us to compare ourselves with other believers. Think of how many hours in prayer they've undoubtedly put in. Think of all the years they've walked with the Lord. Maybe they're twenty years ahead of you spiritually, maybe thirty. Don't be discouraged. God calls you to start right where you are, today. You can begin to learn to hear God's voice. And if you ever doubt, then go again to John 10. God is the Good Shepherd. We're His sheep. He speaks. We listen.

3. Our Ability to Hear God Can Mature

Children learn to speak better and better as they become older. As adults, hopefully, we even learn the art of keeping our mouths shut—and why that can be a big part of communication too. I mean, have you ever noticed how kids just sort of say anything that pops into their mouths? ("Wow, do you ever look old, Grandma. You're ancient! How old are you anyway?")

Here's my point. We can all learn how God communicates with us. But we need to mature in this ability too. For instance, we might say things that come from our religious backgrounds and claim that those things came from God, but maybe God didn't say those things at all.

One Sunday after church many years ago, we were in the lobby of a crowded restaurant, waiting to be seated for lunch, and I noticed a small boy milling about by a cigarette machine. (That's how you know it was long ago—the restaurant still had a cigarette machine in its lobby.) A man came up and bought a pack of cigarettes, and the little boy watched him the whole time. When the man started to walk away, the little boy yelled over to his father, "Hey Daddy! That man just bought cigarettes. He's going to hell!"

Now, I can say with good assurance that smoking may not be the best thing for a person, health-wise. But I can also tell you with good assurance that nowhere does the Bible say that if you buy cigarettes, you are going to hell. See, the little boy was saying things that came from his religious background, but it wasn't the same as if he'd heard those things from God. We need to become mature in our ability to hear the voice of God. But how does this happen?

Becoming Mature Sheep

Let's examine that last idea, how we must mature in our ability to hear God.

Dallas Willard (author and professor of philosophy at the University of Southern California from 1964 to 2012) describes how one philosophy of hearing God is known as "a message a minute," and this method, while it sounds spiritual, is typically immature. This is when people insist that they hear God speak to them a thousand times a day.[1]

It is certainly admirable to "pray continually" as Paul describes in 1 Thessalonians 5:17 (NIV). But when I'm around people who claim to hear a message a minute from God, I have my doubts that this is what is actually going on. They say things like, "You know, God just told me right now not to put salt on my food."

And I think, *Yeah. But you could have read last month's* Reader's Digest *and figured that out.*

Another problem I've seen with the message-a-minute crowd is that they make mistakes. They claim that God speaks to them moment by moment every moment of the day. But my suspicion is what's actually happening is that as any old thought flits through their minds, they grab hold of that thought and falsely label it as a word from the Lord.

Here's an example of how this might flesh out. A man may come up to me after a Sunday service with a frown on his face, and say, "Pastor Robert, God just told me that you're supposed to wear a tie whenever you preach, and if you don't wear a tie, then you're in sin. And God told me that underneath your suit jacket, you're supposed to wear white shirts only, not colored shirts. And God also told me that the congregation of this church is supposed to stop singing worship songs in our services. Instead, from here on out, God wants us to divide ourselves into two groups and chant antiphonally. And, oh yeah, God also wants me to preach here at Gateway for the next five Sundays, instead of you, because He told me I have the gift of teaching."

Now, his message to me is a problem because 2 Corinthians 13:1 says, "By the mouth of two or three witnesses every word shall be established." As senior pastor, I'm under the authority of a group of godly elders, and we're all regularly seeking the Lord and reading Scripture and seeking His face and His voice and His presence, and God didn't tell us any of those things. So I'm going to go out on a limb here and say that this man didn't truly hear from God. What he thought he heard from God about those things is actually a mistake.

Ask yourself this: Do you really want God to speak to you a thousand times a day about every tiny decision you make and every miniscule action you take? Now, I certainly believe in staying in constant communion with God, and I believe in following the directive of 1 Thessalonians 5:17 to "pray without ceasing," and I believe in living our lives and making decisions based on God's Word. But maybe the question is better framed like this: Do you think that God wants to have that type of babyish relationship with you? Is there any parent who wants to have that type of relationship with his children—particularly as they grow to adulthood?

Of course not. A parent wants his or her children to grow up and become mature. Part of maturity means making decisions independently. That's not to say that we ever ignore God or make large decisions independently of Him. But it does mean that we don't need to ask God about what color of shirt to wear for the day. God speaks, absolutely. But we need to grow up too. Hebrews 5:13–14 says, "For everyone who partakes only of milk is unskilled in the word of righteousness, for he is a babe. But solid food belongs to those who are of full age, that is, those who by reason of use have their senses exercised to discern both good and evil."

Another thing we need to be wary of is any can't-fail method or formula to hearing the voice of God. If someone insists he has found a formula whereby you can always hear God, then watch out. Hearing God is all about having a real relationship with Him. Sometimes people open their Bibles at random, point to a verse, and claim it's from the Lord directly for their situation. And, yes, sometimes God may speak that way (we'll talk about this more in a chapter to come). But more often than not, that's a method to take with a grain of salt.

I've heard people insist that every believer can get his life verse by using "the birthday method." That's when you take the numbers of the year, month, and day you were born, and apply them directly to the Bible as chapter, book, and verse. People hold to different theories as to what number of your birthday—month, day, or year—should correspond to which part of the Bible—chapter, book, or verse—because if you were born after 1950, then it's hard to find a chapter that has more than fifty verses in it. So that's another problem with the method. My friend tried this method just to see what would happen. He was born in January, the first month of the year, in 1935, which sounded straightforward. So he went to the Bible and looked in the first book, Genesis, chapter 19, verse 35. In essence it says, "So they got him drunk and slept with him."

Okay, my point is simple: you don't need to be mystical to get a word from God. But you know what all these crazy methods do show us?—and this I actually love. These crazy methods show us that people are genuinely hungry to hear from God. And that's why I'm writing this chapter. The promise is shown clearly when we come back to John 10. God is the Good Shepherd. And His sheep hear His voice.

One more methodology for hearing God bears examination: *Que Sera, Sera,* Spanish for "Whatever will be, will be." It's a methodology that sees widespread usage and is held by people ranging from casual Christians to some seminary professors. It's basically that you choose whatever direction you want to go, and it'll all work out in the end. God gives us complete freedom to make decisions, and so He empowers us with wisdom and discernment and sets us loose.

Certainly the Bible makes it clear that there's a nonspecific will of God. We call this God's general will, and it's taught by Jesus in places such as John 14:21: "He who has My commandments and keeps them, it is he who loves Me. And he who loves Me will be loved by My Father, and I will love him and manifest Myself to him." This passage doesn't contain any specific directives other than to love God. It's a general command, not a detailed plan, and there's much room within the plan for us to act according to our own discernment.

The general will of God is for everyone. A similar general command is given in Matthew 28:19–20, sometimes called the Great Commission, where Jesus tells His disciples, us included, that we're to go and "make disciples of all the nations, baptizing them in the name of the Father and of the Son and of the Holy Spirit, teaching them to observe all things that I have commanded you." Elsewhere in Scripture, God tells us to be filled with the Holy Spirit (Eph. 5:17–18), to be thankful for all things (5:19–20), to separate ourselves from sin and be sanctified (1 Thess. 4:3–7), and to be conformed to the image of God's Son (Rom. 8:28–29). These instructions all fit into the category of God's general will for our lives.

Without doing a full rebuttal of those who believe that a general will is all that God ever gives us, let me just point out that the Bible also describes many occasions of specific calls upon people's lives. For instance, in Genesis 12, Abram is told by God to leave everything familiar and go to a new land. That was God's specific call on Abram's life. In Acts 9, Saul was given a specific calling while on the Damascus road—initially, all it involved was to go to the house of a man named Ananias. If God guided His servants in specific manners in times past, then why would God not guide His servants specifically in present times—particularly in light of John 10? I've seen this to be a reality in my own life, and I know that many other Christians have as well.

Every one of us has major decisions to make in our lives, when we need to hear God. God gives His general counsel, and He also graciously gives us specific counsel. It comes back to the foundational truth set forth in John 10. We are sheep. Jesus is the Good Shepherd. We were designed to hear the voice of God.

God's Voice on a Hike

A friend of mine, fresh out of seminary, received a job offer to be a youth pastor. Initially my friend didn't want to take the job, and part of the reason was that the church was small, and the area around the church was rural. He'd pictured himself ministering in a cool, big-city church, a job he'd imagined would lead to bigger and greater things for the sake of God's kingdom.

Before my friend answered with a no, he had the good sense to take a week, pray about the decision, and listen for the voice of God. He phoned his father, a pastor, and his father directed him to the same portion of Scripture we've discussed all through this chapter—John 10. His father reassured him that God is, indeed, the Good Shepherd, and we can have confidence that when we listen to Him, we can hear His voice.

My friend went for a hike out in the wilderness, and he began to talk to God in prayer, asking the Lord to show him whether he should take the job. He confessed to the Lord his reservations about the size and location of the church. My friend's ambitions were noble and well intentioned. He read missionary biographies that showed how in decades past great men of God did great things for the sake of God's kingdom, and my friend wanted to do similar things with his life.

As he was hiking and praying, this verse came to mind, "Therefore humble yourselves under the mighty hand of God, that He may exalt you in due time" (1 Peter 5:6).

This verse settled in my friend's mind and nested there, and he meditated on God's truth, letting the words of Scripture apply to his situation. Along with that verse, my friend sensed a new and deep peace from God. On the surface, the job didn't appear to be his dream job, but he had fresh perspective about it now, and he sensed strongly that God wanted him there. He considered the verse to be the answer to his prayers, the voice of God for the situation. Part of my friend's particular calling was to humble himself—and God would lift him up in due time.

My friend worked at that church for six years and did a good job, and then the Lord led him on to other things. More than twenty years have passed since then, and today my friend is ministering alongside some of the most influential pastors in America.

That won't be everybody's story, nor would everybody want that. The point is that God guides. His sheep hear His voice. And He calls His own sheep by name and leads them out.

That's what God promises to you.

CHAPTER TWO

WHY HEAR FROM GOD?

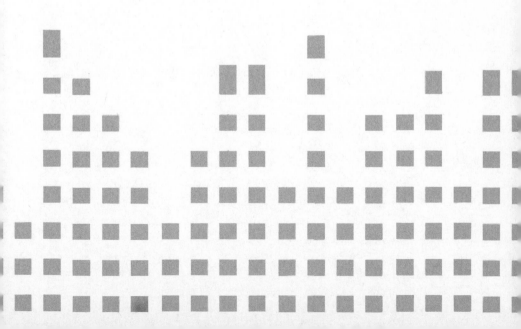

I have called you friends, for all things that I heard
from My Father I have made known to you.
—John 15:15

Let's say I have a friend in the hospital, and he's been there three days. He calls me up and leaves a message: "Hey Robert, I'm lonely and bored, and I'm feeling pretty discouraged. Would you come visit me? Maybe bring some books too, please?"

So I get his message and gather up some books and take them to the hospital. But instead of visiting his room directly, I leave the books at the front desk with a note attached with his name on it. Then I leave. I've fulfilled the request that he asked of me. But if that's all I did, what kind of a friend to him would you say I am?

Here's another situation. Same scenario, same request. But this time I get his message and go to the hospital with a bag of books and then head up to my friend's room. I also bring him some CDs to listen to and some sort of food that I know he loves to eat, maybe a hot cheeseburger and fries if he's well enough to eat that. Or maybe it's a spinach salad with skinless chicken chunks if he's interested in his heart health. I spend as much time with him as he's able to handle, just talking and communicating and sharing our hearts. Sometimes we're silent together, as good friends can be. We're comfortable and familiar in each other's presence. The whole time he's in the hospital, I go spend time with him like this twice a day. I go in the morning before work, and I go in the evening after work. We sit and talk and spend time together like that. Again, I've fulfilled the request that he asked of me. But which of the two scenarios would you say indicates a deeper level of friendship?

The second does, obviously. In the first scenario, it's not that I'm a bad friend necessarily. It's just that our friendship is limited. Maybe I don't know this person very well. Or maybe I do know this person well, and our friendship is shallow or superficial or strained or distant. But with the second scenario, our friendship is rich and deep. We care about each other. We have a lot of things to talk about. We dialogue together and clearly enjoy each other's presence.

Here's the kicker: Guess which kind of friendship God desires with us?

He offers us a rich and deep relationship, like the relationship shown in the second scenario. He offers us a conversational friendship, wherein we both talk to each other. He doesn't just drop off something for us to read and then leave. He doesn't want us to approach Him halfheartedly—with our minds elsewhere—because that's certainly not how He approaches us. He doesn't want us to come to Him simply when we're needy, only approaching Him when we bring a list of requests. He wants a friendship wherein we're close to Him and He's close to us, a friendship that means we're comfortable in each other's presence, and our communication is built around true relationship.

Here's my point: too many times we approach God as though He's some sort of great cosmic Santa Claus. We're distant and removed, and our only motive is to get something from Him. With God, we only want to receive blessing or direction or instruction from Him. Yet God wants something far greater than that. He wants to get to know us, and He desires for us to get to know Him.

Part of the big question I'm raising in this book is, "How can we hear God?" Yet there is another question that goes right along with it, a question that uncovers our hearts before the Lord. It's a question of motivation, a question that digs into the possibility for real relationship. It's this: Why hear from God?

What is our motivation in wanting to hear God's voice? Why do we even care?

The Answer Is Friendship

Someone might argue that the illustration of the hospital visit breaks down because God is not our equal—and this critique is valid. There's no way a mere mortal can fully relate to the limitless God of the universe. The friendship to which God calls us is never a friendship where we're buddies in a casual or irreverent sort of way. God is always God, and we are always human. And God always needs to be seen in our minds and hearts as the Great King.

We call this concept of God's loftiness the doctrine of transcendence—and it's a wonderful doctrine. It means that God is higher, higher than, well, anything we can think of. It means that God is superior, immense, and unequaled—and we always need to keep this doctrine in mind when we approach Him. Psalm 97:9 says, "For You, LORD, are most high above all the earth; You are exalted far above all gods."

Yet hand in glove with the doctrine of transcendence is the doctrine of immanence. This means that God is close to us. He is near. He is relational. He's actively involved in creation. Matthew 1:23 says, "'Behold, the virgin shall be with child, and bear a Son, and they shall call His name Immanuel,' which is translated 'God with us.'"

At first glance those two doctrines sound opposite of each other, but they're actually not. God is both transcendent and immanent at the same time. He is both the Great King and "God with us." We must never forget His greatness, yet it's also true that we never need to keep our distance from God because of the blood of Jesus Christ.

Did you ever see that old classic photograph of John Kennedy Jr. as a little boy in the White House? He's three or four years old, and his father, the president of the United States, is busy in the Oval Office. Yet JFK Jr. is happily playing as only a little boy can do, and he's under the president's desk. That's a picture of transcendence and immanence.

On one hand you have the president of the United States, arguably the world's most powerful person, doing his job. Dignitaries line up to meet him, and if you're in the presence of the president, then you can never forget he's the president. Yet the president is close enough to his son that his son can approach him any time he wishes. The son delights in the father's presence, and the father delights in the son. There's power in the father's position and character. Yet there's also closeness with his children.

It's from these two foundational characteristics of transcendence and immanence that God invites us into a true friendship with Him. We always need to keep in mind the greatness of the Person to whom we're talking and relating. Yet we never need to think that God just drops off a bag of books (even sixty-six wonderful, inspired books in the Bible) at the front counter of the hospital and then leaves. God's not that kind of a friend to us.

In John 15:15, Jesus spells it out for us this way: "No longer do I call you servants, for a servant does not know what his master is doing; but I have called you friends, for all things that I heard from My Father I have made known to you."

This is such a wonderful truth for us. God, the great God of the universe, calls us His friends. Here's the same verse in the New Living Translation, a thought-by-thought rendering of the original language: "I no longer call you slaves, because a master doesn't confide in his slaves. Now you are my friends, since I have told you everything the Father told me."

Jesus is saying that a master doesn't confide in his slaves, but a friend tells another friend what's going on. This is the type of relationship Jesus makes available to us. (By the way, this doesn't mean that Jesus tells us everything right away. He says later that there are other things He wants to say to us, but He's not going to say them. The Holy Spirit is going to say them. But I'm getting ahead of myself here.)

So in this passage Jesus opens the door to establish a deep level of friendship with us. He has come that we might have a right relationship with the Father, and part of that relationship involves communication. He has told us what the Father has told Him.

Let's examine this scriptural truth in light of the question I raised at the start of the chapter, why hear from God? What follows are three truths that answer this question of motivation and show what this friendship is like.

1. God Does Not Speak to Robots

God does not speak to robots. Here's what I mean: God didn't create us to mindlessly obey His commands. He created us as persons. We have souls, (minds, wills, emotions,) and hearts. God wants to communicate with us personally because He gave us personalities, and He Himself has personality. Only a personal connection will do.

Have you ever thought about how we communicate to machines—and how machines communicate with us? A car is a machine. If we want to communicate with a car, we give it an order. If we want it to go faster, we press the accelerator pedal. If we want it to go slower, we press the brakes. If we want to make a right turn off the main road and head into a donut shop (*ahem*—or a healthy salad place), we turn the steering wheel to the right. It's mechanical communication. We give the machine an order, and it obeys.

Some of us even have cars today that talk back to us. But this is not a true dialogue. I'm referring to the voice of the GPS system. I have one of these in my car, and I can tell you that the voice of a woman who speaks from my GPS is cold. In fact, she always sounds as if she's annoyed with me, constantly telling me I'm doing something wrong. I'm almost positive last week I heard her sigh with disgust and say, "Recalculating . . . you dummy!"

To be clear, the voice of my GPS is not actually talking to me.

Someone programmed the computer in the GPS to say those words. And actually the voice is not capable of emotion at all, not even annoyance. When we communicate with a computer, we press keys and click a mouse, and then it does whatever it is told to do. God did not create us so that His relationship to us is like our relationships to machines. God did not create us as robots. Instead, He created us as His children. And in a personal way God communicates with the children He created. There are no lines or mazes we have to navigate in order to talk with our Father. He invites us to come to Him anytime. We can even play, as it were, in His office under His desk.

One of the greatest ways a human is seen to have a friendship with God is displayed in the example of Abraham. James 2:23 says, "And the Scripture was fulfilled which says, 'Abraham believed God, and it was accounted to him for righteousness.' And *he was called the friend of God*."

In Genesis 18 Abraham had a true dialogue with God. Abraham initially talked with three visitors (one is the angel of the Lord) about the son that God had promised to Abraham in his old age. The three visitors and Abraham enjoyed a meal together along with a quiet, peaceful, hospitable exchange. Then the conversation shifted. A great outcry had arisen against Sodom and Gomorrah, two ancient cities known for their perversity and rebellion, and the Lord had decided that He was going to destroy the two cities because of the citizens' wickedness. Then the two men left, "but Abraham still stood before the LORD. And Abraham came near" (Gen. 18:22–23).

In this short verse we see a pattern for true communication established. Abraham stopped what he was doing and drew near to God. This pattern is true for us as well. If we want to hear from the Lord, then we, too, must stop what we are doing and draw close to God.

Once Abraham had drawn near, we see one of the most amazing conversations unfold as Abraham negotiated with God. First, Abraham asked a question of God:

"Would You also destroy the righteous with the wicked? Suppose there were fifty righteous within the city; would You also destroy the place and not spare it for the fifty righteous that were in it? Far be it from You to do such a thing as this, to slay the righteous with the wicked, so that the righteous should be as the wicked; far be it from You! Shall not the Judge of all the earth do right?" (vv. 23–25)

It's a strange conversation because Abraham knew that God would never do wrong. And of course, God, by nature of His holy and righteous character, would indeed never do anything wrong. But still Abraham felt that he needed to remind God of this. Abraham knew God well enough to know that unjust actions weren't in God's character. Of course, God hadn't forgotten this. Rather, it's almost as if Abraham needed to remind himself of this truth while he was in God's presence.

The Lord said, "If I find in Sodom fifty righteous within the city, then I will spare all the place for their sakes" (v. 26).

The negotiations continued. Abraham answered, "Indeed now, I who am but dust and ashes have taken it upon myself to speak to the Lord: Suppose there were five less than the fifty righteous; would You destroy all of the city for lack of five?" (vv. 27–28). Note how this is an example of transcendence and immanence coming into play. Abraham acknowledged the sheer audacity of what he was doing—a mere man like him, who is but dust and ashes, had taken it upon himself to speak to God. God is lofty and mighty. But God is also near and close. Abraham was reverent in how he communicated with God. Yet Abraham was also familiar with God.

And God lowered the requirements to forty-five.

Then Abraham asked for forty.

And God said okay, forty.

Then Abraham asked for thirty.

And God said okay, thirty.

Then Abraham asked for twenty.

And God said okay, twenty.

Then, when we get to verse 32, Abraham asked for ten.

And God said okay, for the sake of ten righteous people in Sodom, he would not destroy the city.

Here's what I believe happened in that interchange: Abraham had previously rescued the people of Sodom in battle (Gen. 14:16) because it was the city where his nephew, Lot, lived. As a wise and compassionate man, Abraham cared about these people. He hoped the best for them. So he was praying for them, interceding on their behalf, even though he knew the city was rotten and that Lot should live someplace else. Abraham wasn't trying to change God's mind as much as he was trying to sort out the justice of God's plan.

> Really Lord, that's really what You want to do? That's what Your justice looks like? Let me just try to get my mind around this.

That's the kind of conversation the Lord invites us to have with Him. God doesn't destroy wicked cities today as He did with Sodom and Gomorrah back then, but God's justice still exists.

> Really Lord, is there such a place called hell? And will people who have turned from Your face actually spend eternity in hell, away from Your presence? Really, Lord—is that what justice looks like? God, if so, then I desperately pray for my unsaved friends and family members. Please, Lord, let them hear the gospel. Let them open their hearts to Jesus. Thank You that You are always just and merciful. Amen.

That type of prayer is not a robot prayer. We're not merely taking orders from God; we're dialoguing about His actions and character, seeking to understand Him, and seeking to intercede on behalf of others. God isn't changing His mind because of our prayers, but He's inviting us into the process with Him. He does not simply input data into our lives to get the results He wants. We're invited to pray as a dialogue with God, one where we hear God's voice, and where God brings understanding to our hearts and minds. This is when we have a true friendship with God.

2. God Speaks to People

The second truth that shows what a friendship with God is like is the straightforward truth that God speaks to people. I know this seems elementary, but it bears closer examination.

God speaks to people. Just roll that truth around in your mind a bit. Get your mind around the startling wonder of that fact.

God . . .

speaks . . .

. . . to people!

He spoke to people in the Bible. And He still speaks to people today. I believe He even uses much the same method, which I'll discuss in greater detail in a few pages.

When we look at Scripture, it's easy to see that God spoke to people throughout the Bible. God spoke to Adam and Eve in the cool of the day in the garden of Eden. God spoke to Noah, Moses, Abraham, Isaac, Jacob, Deborah, Ruth, and more. In the New Testament, God spoke to Peter, Paul, James, John, Luke, Jude—and even Cornelius, the Roman centurion. Have you ever thought about that? Cornelius wasn't even a follower of Christ initially, yet he still heard the voice of God (Acts 10). That's how much God cares for people. He's constantly speaking to people, always inviting them to draw a step closer to Him.

God speaks to us today because of the indwelling of the Holy Spirit. In John 16:12–13, Jesus is talking to His disciples and says, "I still have many things to say to you, but you cannot bear them now. However, when He, the Spirit of truth, has come, He will guide you into all truth; for He will not speak on His own authority, but whatever He hears He will speak; and He will tell you things to come."

Who is going to speak to you? The Holy Spirit.

Who is going to tell you of things to come? The Holy Spirit.

Although God finished His formal revelation when He gave us the Bible two thousand years ago, God did not finish speaking two thousand years ago. He said,

I'm telling you that you are My friends. Do you know the one big reason how you can know you're My friends? Because I tell you things! A master doesn't tell his slaves things. An engineer doesn't tell his machine things. But you are My friends, and I will tell you things. I won't leave you as orphans. I'm going to send someone to you—the Holy Spirit—and He is going to tell you those things.

How does God speak? Sometimes we have this idea in mind that the way God spoke to people in the Bible was through a big booming voice—there was no way they could ever miss it. It would be impossible not to know that the voice was God's. They couldn't mistake that voice. And if God only spoke to us today in that same big, booming, Charlton Heston–type voice, then all would be okay. Right?

I'm not so sure it was that way back in the Bible. Certainly God's voice was clear when He inspired men to write Scripture. "No prophecy of Scripture is of any private interpretation, for prophecy never came by the will of man, but holy men of God spoke as they were moved by the Holy Spirit" (2 Peter 1:20–21).

But how did God talk to people in the Bible when He just wanted to have a dialogue with them? The story of Elijah in the wilderness shows that God sometimes chose to speak in a still small voice (1 Kings 19). After escaping from the clutches of wicked queen Jezebel, Elijah ran for his life into the wilderness and collapsed under a broom tree. Elijah was exhausted and disheartened, and he prayed that he might die. But an angel told him to get up, have a drink of water and a meal of bread baked on coals to refresh himself, and then journey for forty days to Horeb, the mountain of God. There, Elijah went into a cave, where the Lord began to dialogue with him as one would talk with a friend.

> [God] said to him, "What are you doing here, Elijah?"
>
> So [Elijah] said [from inside the cave], "I have been very zealous for the LORD God of hosts; for the children of Israel have forsaken Your covenant, torn down Your altars, and killed Your prophets with the sword. I alone am left; and they seek to take my life."
>
> Then [God] said, "Go out, and stand on the mountain before the LORD." And behold, the LORD passed by, and a great and strong wind tore into the mountains and broke the rocks in pieces before the LORD, but the LORD was not in the wind; and after the wind an earthquake, but the LORD was not in the earthquake; and after the earthquake a fire, but the LORD was not in the fire; and after the fire a still small voice.
>
> So it was, when Elijah heard it, that he wrapped his face in his mantle and went out and stood in the entrance of the cave. (1 Kings 19:9–13)

How did God speak to this man Elijah? Not in a big, booming voice. Not in a strong wind, or in an earthquake, or in a fire. But in a still small voice—"a gentle whisper" (v. 12 NIV).

I wonder if that was the same as what we'd call today an impression on our hearts. God impressed what He wanted to say upon Elijah's heart. We don't know for certain which method God chose to use. But maybe a still small voice is tantamount to the prompting of the Holy Spirit.

Consider the example in Scripture of God speaking to another man, Gideon (Judg. 6). God showed up and spoke to Gideon, but Gideon was unsure about the message—so unsure that he twice tested God by putting out a fleece. Do you know why Gideon wanted to do that? His uncertainty is very clear. In Judges 6:17, Gideon said to God, "Show me a sign that it is You who talk with me."

Why did Gideon doubt God's voice? If God had spoken to him in a big, booming voice, then why was Gideon so uncertain about the voice?

I'm going to suggest that maybe God did not speak to Gideon in a big, booming voice as we often imagine. I think that God spoke to Gideon in a still small voice, the same kind of voice that He used to speak to Elijah in the cave at Horeb. I think God might have even impressed the message upon Gideon's heart, the same as He does for us today.

Why would I suggest such a thing? It's because of Hebrews 11, the great "hall of faith" chapter in the Bible. In Hebrews 11, person after person is listed, all friends of God: Enoch, Noah, Abraham, Sarah, Isaac, Jacob, Moses, Rahab, Gideon, Barak, Samson, Jephthah, David, Samuel, and on and on.

All these people heard from God. And all these people lived by faith.

Every person who has ever heard the voice of God has needed to act in faith. And some of these people even had Scripture too. Moses had the recorded words of God at his disposal. The New Testament believers had the law, the Psalms, and the writings of the prophets. They were constantly quoting from Scripture, saying, "It is written, it is written, it is written." God spoke to them in addition to the Scripture they already had. And yet they all still needed to live by faith.

When God speaks to you today, chances are that He won't speak to you in a big, booming voice. Instead, God will speak to you by the moving of the Holy Spirit in your life (John 16:12–13). He'll speak to you by His still small voice. And what you do after He speaks to you will require faith.

3. God Speaks to Friends

The third truth that shows what a friendship with God is like is the biblical examination of the very truth that God does indeed speak to friends. God does not speak to robots. He speaks with people. And He speaks with people as a man speaks to his friend. How do we know this? Look at two foundational verses:

> So the LORD spoke to Moses face to face, as a man speaks to his friend.
>
> —Exodus 33:11

> And the Scripture was fulfilled which says, "Abraham believed God, and it was accounted to him for righteousness." And he was called the friend of God.
>
> —James 2:23

We must begin to grasp this wonderful truth that God desires to be our friend, just as God was a friend of Moses. If we don't grasp this, then we will be apt to communicate with God only when we are in trouble, or when we've got a big decision to make, or when we want something from Him. God wants to be our friend. He wants to talk to us every day.

Friendship with God is an awesome privilege. It's also an awesome responsibility, one we are not to take lightly. Remember who else was a friend of God?

Judas.

> Now His betrayer had given them a sign, saying, "Whomever I kiss, He is the One; seize Him." Immediately he went up to Jesus and said, "Greetings, Rabbi!" and kissed Him.
>
> *But Jesus said to him, "Friend, why have you come?"*

Then they came and laid hands on Jesus and took Him. (Matt. 26:48–50)

Do you sense the gravity of Jesus' question to Judas? Right in front of Jesus is the man who betrays Him, yet Jesus still calls him a friend. Jesus' question is an echo of a conversation with his disciples that began earlier:

"Greater love has no one than this, than to lay down one's life for his friends. You are My friends if you do whatever I command you. No longer do I call you servants, for a servant does not know what his master is doing; but I have called you friends, for all things that I heard from My Father I have made known to you." (John 15:13–15)

If we are disciples of Jesus, then we are friends of God. Jesus lays down His life for His friends. He lays down His life for us—even when we betray Him, even when we sin.

Friendship with God is at the core of the gospel message. I love how the New Living Translation words Romans 5:10, "For since our friendship with God was restored by the death of his Son while we were still his enemies, we will certainly be saved through the life of his Son."

Think of your best friend on earth. There are no formalities with this friend, no fear with this person, and no rituals to perform or special language to use. The relationship you have with each other is deep and close. Because of the work that Jesus did on the cross for us, Jesus restored us to friendship with God. "All this is done by God, who through Christ changed us from enemies into his friends" (2 Cor. 5:18 GNT).

An old hymn is titled "What a Friend We Have in Jesus." Technically, we are friends with all three members of the Trinity—Father, Son, and Holy Spirit—yet the spirit of that song still rings true. With God, we can go to Him with all our sins and griefs, and He will bear them. He offers us peace, not fear. He invites us to come to Him in the midst of our trials and temptations. When we are weak and heavy laden, He says, *Hey, I'm your Friend. I'll help you and keep you. Trust in Me.* He restores us to friendship with Him, even in the midst of our sin.

Better Than Presents

My son James has loved fishing all his life. One year, when James was about nine, we planned as a family to take some time off and travel to the home of Debbie's parents. They lived about three hours away in another part of Texas and had a pond on their land. James was particularly looking forward to catching some large-mouth bass in their pond.

Debbie and the children left on Friday afternoon to travel over there, but I stayed for Saturday and Sunday services, planning to join my family later on Sunday afternoon.

On Saturday evening when I phoned Debbie, she indicated that I needed to talk to James and ask him how his day went. So I did. James had the best day fishing ever. He was so excited. He'd caught fish all day, one after another, and I promised him that the next day when I arrived, we'd go fishing together.

Sunday after church, I stopped at a bait store, bought James a lure I knew he'd wanted, and then headed over to my in-laws. I gave James his present, and he said thanks. Then he and I fished all the rest of that day.

Well, you know how fishing goes. We fished, and we fished, and we fished, but those bass had stopped biting because James and I didn't catch a thing.

At the end of the day, I said, "James, I'm sorry that today wasn't as good a day as it was for you yesterday."

He looked at me kind of strangely, then smiled in sincerity, and said, "Dad, today was much better than yesterday."

"How come?" I asked.

"Because today you were here with me."

That's a picture of us and God. Dallas Willard talks about how God extends the invitation to us to treasure His presence more than His presents.[1] I like that a lot. My son James may have been grateful for the present I gave him of the fishing lure, but he was happier to spend time with me, to enjoy being in my presence. After more than thirty-five years of walking with the Lord, God has blessed me in more ways than I could ever mention. I understand how He has blessed my family so greatly—and I'm thankful for that. But even more than God's blessings and gifts, I've learned to treasure God's presence. This is a really foundational truth with huge practical implications.

One morning I was praying, and I found myself approaching God with my to-do list. Have you ever done the same thing? I was giving God my list of things that He needed to do while I did my things for the day.

And just like that, God kind of broke into the prayer and impressed upon my heart,

Hey Robert, can we just be in each other's presence for a while? Can we just hang out together? I know you're concerned about all these things on your list. But everything's going to be okay there. Let me remind you of a few scriptures to set your heart at ease. "Before they call, I will answer." And "My God shall supply all your need according to His riches in glory by Christ Jesus." I'm going to take care of your list. Don't worry. But let's just talk today. (Isa. 65:24; Phil. 4:19)

And so we did.

In John 15:15, Jesus says that He calls us His friends because He communicates to us what the Father has told Him. God's primary motive for speaking to us is not to input information or to give us directives to be followed. He speaks to us because He wants us to be His friends. God designed us to communicate with Him on a personal level and in a personal way. Since the beginning of time, He has been speaking personally and specifically to people, and He has never changed.

We are invited to take hold of that glorious truth that God wants to be our friend. Otherwise, we will only want to hear Him because of selfish motives. When we pursue God because we want to know Him, rather than to just get something from Him, we will also come to understand what He wants us to do. He wants us to treasure His presence more than His presents.

Imagine yourself sitting with God, having coffee and chatting about life as you might with a friend. What kinds of things would you talk about that you aren't currently talking to Him about right now?

Here's my invitation to you today. Thank God for His desire for friendship with you. Thank Him for making Himself available to be your friend. Ask Him to show you steps to take so that you can open your heart to Him this way. Pray for any obstacles to be removed that may be hindering your friendship with God.

Why hear the voice of God? God wants to be your friend!

How awesome is that thought!

CHAPTER THREE

GO TO THE BIBLE

Your word is a lamp to my feet
And a light to my path.
—Psalm 119:105

I felt like a kid.

Truly I did. When I was thirty, I was an associate pastor at a growing church. I'd become a Christian at age nineteen, and in the eleven years since then, I'd done a lot of growing up spiritually, but in many ways I still felt young in my faith. I didn't feel like a grown-up. Yet new, grown-up responsibilities were being handed to me, and I didn't know what to do.

The new responsibility being held out to me was a job offer. We had multiple congregations, but those were the days before simulcasts, and we had a preaching pastor at each campus. When we'd grown to have five campuses, the senior pastor decided to put a different pastor at the mother church and move himself to a senior position over all the campuses. It was a good idea, and that way he would be able to better shepherd all the campuses. So he prayed about it and asked me to become the pastor of the mother church campus.

Gulp.

I wasn't ready to undertake such a weighty role—at least I didn't think so. It was sort of a funny twist of events to me because five years earlier, when I was the ripe old age of twenty-five, I was firmly convinced I was ready for the responsibility. But I'd matured a bit over time, and the older I got, the more I knew what it would take to be a campus pastor. At age thirty I couldn't imagine myself with all that responsibility on my shoulders.

The clock was ticking. I needed to give my pastor an answer. If it were solely up to me, I would have immediately said no to my pastor's request. But in the spirit of Proverbs 3:5–6, I didn't want to lean on my own understanding. I wanted to hear God's thoughts on the matter. I needed to hear God's voice. Ultimately, I wanted to love, serve, and obey God, and even though I was shaking in my boots about the new job opening, if Jesus wanted me to take the new job, then I would follow Him and take it.

So I went away by myself for a time to devote myself to seeking the Lord's face and hearing His voice. I worshipped, prayed, wrote down my prayers, and more keenly entered the presence of the Lord. I asked the Lord to guide me using the Bible, and I distinctly felt the Holy Spirit impressing me to read Luke 3. That passage kept coming back to mind, Luke 3, Luke 3, Luke 3.

I turned there, began to read, and came to verse 23: "Now Jesus Himself began His ministry at about thirty years of age."

I stopped cold. I read the verse again.

Thirty.

Jesus would be guiding me along this pathway. Leading the church campus wasn't my responsibility ultimately. It was His. My responsibility was to stay close to Him, to continue to immerse myself in His Word and prayer, and to devote myself to serving Him. He would guide. He would protect. This was the confirmation I was looking for. A peace that passes understanding came over me. The confirmation was felt deep in my heart.

I wonder what you need today.

Do you need to hear God's voice?

Maybe it's for guidance, renewal, conviction, wisdom, or confirmation, or for a fresh vision of the way forward or a strong reassurance of God's love. These and more are all found in a person. And to meet this person, the place to start is by reading the book He wrote: the Bible.

We live in a dark world, and we will stumble directionally unless we regularly switch on the bright light of God's Word. God's Word acts as a lamp and sheds light on the way we should go. It shows us how we should walk. It shows us which directions to turn so we avoid pitfalls.

It provides a road map of wisdom, a wellspring of hope, and a limitless fountain of the assurance of His love. The Holy Spirit uses the words of Scripture to gently impress upon us truths we need to learn and heed.

Ultimately, God's Word shows us that He is a person. In the Bible, God reveals His identity, His love for us, His grace and mercy toward us, and His overall purpose and plan for our lives and futures. The Bible tells us about God's character, intentions, and actions. It tells us how God walks, talks, and breathes. How He lies down and rises up. How He acts when He moves on something. If we want to know God, then we need to get into His Word. God's Word illuminates our way.

Do you need to hear God's voice?

Start by reading your Bible.

A Lamp and a Light

Maybe you've woken up in the middle of the night and needed to go to the bathroom or wanted to go to the kitchen, and then while you were walking across a dark room, you stubbed your toe. I know I've done this—and it hurts! I bet you've done this too. What will help in a situation like that?

The answer is simple. Turn on a lamp. When we flip on a light switch, there is no argument between light and dark. When the light is on, the darkness is gone. There's no fight. There's no struggle.

Similarly, if we feel confused about which direction to turn, then the first thing we ought to do is turn to God and read the Bible. Go to God through the pages of His Word. King David, in Psalm 119:105, states it plainly: "Your word is a lamp to my feet and a light to my path." Light dispels darkness. First John 1:5 declares this truth: "God is light and in Him is no darkness at all."

A man came to me for counsel a while back. He needed help in the area of sexual purity and said with a frown on his face, "You just don't understand, Pastor, how many horrible things I've seen. The magazines. The movies. The Internet videos and pictures. I've just seen so much darkness I don't know what to do."

I said, "Okay, listen, my friend. Undeniably, you've seen things with your eyes that you shouldn't have seen. But do you understand that if you allow God's light to shine, then God's light will dispel that darkness? It may not happen all at once when darkness is deeply layered over a life, but I'm telling you that if you take the Bible and read God's Word, study God's Word, meditate on God's Word, memorize God's Word, then the light will overcome the darkness. The Bible is the lamp that gets rid of the darkness."

God's voice saves us and cleanses us from sin, and His voice guides our pathways in other areas too. In Luke 15:8, Jesus tells the story of a woman with ten silver coins. She loses one coin and is dismayed at her loss. But then she lights a lamp, sweeps her house, and carefully searches every nook and cranny until she finds the coin. The brightness of the lamp leads to rediscovered value. Nothing important is lost forever with the light of a lamp as our guide.

Have you ever lost something valuable to you—a friendship, a relationship, a marriage, an investment, your health? Maybe you lose your direction and need to refocus your priorities. Maybe one of your children or grandchildren loses her way spiritually, and it feels as though she's lost. Maybe you journey through a season of doubt or depression or grief, and the close relationship with God that you once felt doesn't feel intact anymore. Your faith feels lost.

Here's what Jesus says: when you lose something valuable to you, go light the lamp. Go to the brightness of Scripture. Read God's Word. Ask yourself, "What does the Bible say about this?" In times of loss, certainly you'll be discouraged or grieving. You might be confused about how to go forward or about what to do next. The answer is to go to God's Word.

He will provide comfort and restoration, guidance and hope. God's light will illuminate our paths.

There are so many times in life when I need wisdom, and I wonder where to go or what to do. The imagery of brightness and guidance is found in Daniel 12:3: "Those who are wise will shine like the brightness of the heavens, and those who lead many to righteousness, like the stars forever and ever" (NIV). That verse along with James 1:5 are two of my favorite verses: "If any of you lacks wisdom, you should ask God, who gives generously to all without finding fault, and it will be given to you" (NIV). That answer is so straightforward: ask God, and wisdom will be given to you.

Your invitation is to read God's Word consistently, diligently, prayerfully, and fervently. Read the Bible with your heart wide-open in prayer and in communion with God. Read and pray at the same time:

> Lord Jesus, what are You saying in Your Word about
> Yourself? How does this passage teach me to love You and
> to love others more? How does this passage apply to me?

I love the words that God gave to Joshua:

> Be strong and very courageous. Be careful to obey all the law my
> servant Moses gave you; do not turn from it to the right or to the left,
> that you may be successful wherever you go. Keep this Book of the
> Law always on your lips; meditate on it day and night, so that you may
> be careful to do everything written in it. Then you will be prosperous
> and successful. (Josh. 1:7–8 NIV)

The phrase "meditate on it day and night" is key. When we're seeking God's voice, we're to run scripture through our minds and hearts regularly. That's why I love memorizing scripture so much. Yes, memorizing does take diligence, but what sweet diligence it is. God's Word cleanses our hearts and minds. God's Word sheds light on any darkened corners or shady pathways. God's Word is the lamp that gives brightness and illuminates our pathways.

A Personal Word from God's Word

"Sure, we can read our Bibles," people say. "But how do we know God is speaking to us from within the pages of Scripture for our particular situation? Should we just open the Bible at random, plunk down our finger onto the page, and believe that this is God's voice?"

I know people who use this method, and I never want to limit God from what He can do, but let me just say that this method has its risks. There's an old joke that describes a man who sought God's guidance using the finger-on-the-random-page method. He closed his eyes, let his Bible fall open, and read, "Judas went out and hanged himself." The man shuddered, flipped over a few pages, and read, "Go and do likewise." Now he was really sweating, but he thought he'd give it one more shot, so he plunked his finger down again at random and read, "What you are about to do, do quickly!"

In all seriousness, confusion from using this method occurs in the lives of believers more often than we think. True story: A friend of mine, a businessman, had a business that was suffering, so he went to a seminar with a colleague. The businessman was a believer, and he described to his colleague the journey he'd been on. "Several years ago I opened my Bible and pointed my finger, and the text said, 'cattle.' So I went into cattle. Then a few years later I opened my Bible again like that, put my finger down, and saw 'oil.' So I went into oil." With his business now struggling, my friend had closed his eyes, opened his Bible, and put his finger down. When he opened his eyes, he saw his finger pointed to

"Chapter 11." Not very encouraging words for a guy whose business is failing.

So I'm not recommending that method, particularly as standard practice. Instead, here's what I recommend. Psalm 119:89 (NIV) says that God's Word is "eternal." And Psalm 90:2 tells us that God is timeless, "from everlasting to everlasting." That means if God spoke something three thousand years ago, it is still true today. We can read a verse in the Bible that was written thousands of years ago, and it is still the Word of God today—it is God speaking to mankind. And the Holy Spirit can take that ancient passage and use it to speak to us today about a particular personal matter. As believers, we can have confidence that God is time-less, His Word is eternal, and He can still speak to us about our situation.

Certainly sound principles are needed to interpret and apply Scripture correctly, and we never want to undermine those principles in our quest to hear God's voice. For instance, an Israelite man had an obli-gation to marry his brother's widow and raise up children through her (Deut. 25:5). That's God's civil law, and a law such as that helped shape and guide the Israelites' culture back then, but God doesn't command us to keep that same civil law today. So we need to both take into account the historical and cultural context of a specific passage of Scripture and also realize that the Holy Spirit will give us a word from His living and active Word as He so chooses. And we need to do both at the same time. It's like saying, "Yes, here's the context of the passage, and yes, here's how I believe the Lord spoke to me from this passage," all in the same breath.

Why? The Bible can be both literal and metaphorical at the same time. In John 2:1–11, for instance, when Jesus turned water into wine—that incident literally happened. In the town of Cana in the region of Galilee, at an actual wedding of two real people, Jesus told servants to fill six stone water jars, the kind used by the Jews for ceremonial wash-ing, and Jesus miraculously turned that water into the most robust and refreshing wine anyone had ever tasted.

Two thousand years later we won't be attending the same specific wedding ceremony that Jesus attended in Cana, and the teaching isn't that Jesus will literally turn water into wine at our weddings today. But that passage of Scripture still applies to us—not literally, but metaphorically. It gives us a picture of how Jesus sometimes chooses to work. The principle that Jesus still works miracles is a principle that applies to us today. And the principle that Jesus can take stone-cold jars once used for dead, dull religious ceremonies and fill them with His fresh, vibrant new wine of life is something we all need to hear.

So how do we hear God's voice through the pages of Scripture, taking into account both the historical and cultural contexts and the reality of the Holy Spirit moving in our lives?

Enter God's Presence

The very first thing we need to do is enter the presence of God. Now, I realize that God is omnipresent, so He's always present everywhere, but I'm using this concept of *presence* in the same sense that Psalm 100:4 encourages us to "enter into His gates with thanksgiving, and into His courts with praise. Be thankful to Him, and bless His name." In this sense, the action of entering the presence of God means to cultivate a deliberate awareness of the reality and nearness of God.

I do this personally. I love being outdoors near a lake, so many times I'll go to a lake where I can be alone with the Lord. I'll sit near the shore and turn on some worship music and listen to it. I'll begin worshipping the Lord and enter His presence in the sense of cultivating an awareness of Him. I'll sing and pray and worship until I feel His nearness. When we want to hear God's voice, it's key to spend time worshipping Him first. Whenever we worship the Lord, we open the lines of communication with Him. We come into His presence with singing and into His courts with praise.

When I sense God's nearness, I like to remind myself of the

tremendous truth of Philippians 4:6: "Be anxious for nothing, but in everything by prayer and supplication, with thanksgiving, let your requests be made known to God." It's a verse I recommend that you memorize. It lays out a sequence that can't be ignored. Pray and praise and worship first. Then second, ask. It's as though God is saying in this passage, "Hey, if something's on your heart, tell Me about it. Know that I'm God first. Then if you're concerned about something, tell Me about it. If you have a request, make the request. Go ahead and tell Me what your request is. If you want to talk about your children, then talk. Your marriage, then talk. Your job, then talk. Which job to take, whom to marry, to which school to send your children—whatever is on your mind—then talk." It's absolutely wonderful that the Bible invites us to do this.

One of the best actions I take in this relational process is to write down my prayers. It helps keep my mind focused, and it also gives me a record for future reference of what I've asked of the Lord. Just try it. You might not think you're the world's best writer, and that's fine. The Lord never grades on quality of grammar or handwriting. Tomorrow morning, get up, turn on some worship music, and write out your prayers. It helps us release our thoughts and concerns to the Lord when we can get them out of our minds and hearts and souls and onto paper.

Somewhere in this process of praising the Lord, praying to God, and proclaiming His goodness, you'll begin to sense the Holy Spirit. It's a subjective experience, but it's real nevertheless. This requires sensitivity and carefulness. Maybe you're writing a prayer, asking God to bring good friends into your child's life. Or maybe you're deeply concerned about a friend with a cancer diagnosis. Somewhere in the process you will begin to sense that the Lord is hearing your prayers. You'll remind yourself of the truth in Philippians 4:7, that as you let your requests be made known to God, "the peace of God, which surpasses all understanding, will guard your hearts and minds through Christ Jesus." The Holy

Spirit will bring words into your mind that correspond with Scripture, such as God has "loved you with an everlasting love" (Jer. 31:3), or "Fear not, for I am with you" (Isa. 41:10). It's as if God is saying to you, *I'll take care of this. I have your child in My hands. I have your cancer-ridden friend in My hands. If things are bothering you, know that I am in control. Hey, it's okay. I've got this.* I encourage you to write down these impressions as well. Write down the thoughts that align with God's Word that are encouraging you.

At this point of being in God's presence, I usually open my Bible and begin to read in earnest. It's after I've praised God and prayed and spent time drawing near to Him in worship and prayer. It's after I begin to sense His presence and after sound scriptural thoughts are running through my mind. I don't ignore the context of a passage. I take the context into account while I'm inviting God to speak to me from His Word. This is when I want to see what God will say to me.

Read in a Logical Place

The question inevitably comes up, "Where should I read?" And I think it is fine to have a daily reading plan and simply continue reading that day wherever your plan directs you. If you want to do that, that's okay. But a lot of times when I need a word from God, I pray and ask Him specifically what He wants me to read. I bring Him into the conversation. At that point, either a passage of Scripture will come to mind, or a particular book of the Bible will come to mind, and I'll turn there.

Let's say I'm praying about marriage. Then I'll purposely read about some marriages in the Bible—maybe about Abraham and Sarah, or Isaac and Rebecca, or Jacob and Rachel, or Boaz and Ruth. If I'm wondering about finances, then I'll read some verse on finances or stewardship. If I'm concerned about a health problem, either for myself or for someone else, I'll read some verses on health and healing in the Bible. Again, the specific passage I read sometimes will and sometimes won't literally and directly apply to me. But if it's not a literal application for me, then God will give me principles from the passages that I can still apply to my life.

I encourage you to try this. Maybe you're a woman, and your marriage is in trouble. You don't know what to do about it, so you're seeking a word from the Lord. First, you spend time praising God and entering His presence, and then you ask God where you should read, and maybe the story of Abraham and Sarah comes to mind. As you read through Genesis 12 and 20, you see that Abraham was a godly man, but he still made plenty of mistakes in his marriage. Abraham lied twice about Sarah and was so fearful of neighboring rulers that he was going to let another man sleep with her to save his own neck. So you ask the Lord in prayer,

God, what do You want me to see from this passage?
What is Your word for me here, Lord?

The application isn't literal. You're not married to Abraham, and you don't live in the Canaanite wilderness. You're married to Elwood, and you live in the Peoria suburbs. But the Lord brings to mind 1 Peter 3:6, which talks about Sarah respecting Abraham anyway. The Holy Spirit nudges you in this area, and you realize that no man is perfect, not Abraham, and not your husband. With this knowledge and the power and presence of the Holy Spirit living in you, you are able to respect your husband, flawed though he is.

Or perhaps you're a man and you're also going through marriage problems. Your wife always seems to be nagging you, and her constant complaining is getting to you, so you seek a word from the Lord. First, you spend time praising God and entering His presence, and then you ask God where you should read, and the story of Mary and Martha comes to mind. It's not a marriage story, but as you read the account in Luke 10:38–42, you notice, at first, that the friend of Jesus known as

Martha has a very strong and intense personality, similar to your wife's. In the passage Martha is irritated at her more laid-back sister, Mary, even to the point where Martha complains to Jesus about her. The Holy Spirit begins to nudge you, and you realize that even though your wife is godly and loves Jesus, sometimes a godly woman can be so intense that she misses the more important activity of sitting at the feet of Jesus, as the passage points out.

Then the Lord brings to mind Ephesians 5:25, where husbands are told to love their wives, "just as Christ also loved the church and gave Himself for her." And you realize your job is to love your wife, even when she nags you. Maybe there's a reason for her nagging. Maybe you're leaving your socks around the house. Maybe it's just her beautifully intense personality at work. Maybe it's a combination of both.

You keep prayerfully reading, and the Lord takes you to John 11, where Lazarus dies. He's the brother of Mary and Martha, and in that account we see Martha as a woman of deep sorrow and concern. She's also a woman of tremendous depth and spiritual insight in her conversations with Jesus. You're impressed with her, much the same way that you're impressed, down deep, with your wife. You realize that in spite of your wife's nagging, she has a lot of great qualities too, and you can't ignore those.

You keep reading, and a little later on, in John 12, you see Jesus again in the home of Mary and Martha. Now they're celebrating the resurrection of Lazarus from the dead, and Martha is once again serving, and Mary is once again sitting at the feet of Jesus. But this time there's no mention of complaining from Martha. Her personality has matured. There's joy and fellowship in the house. And the Holy Spirit says to you, *Hey, when it comes to your wife, it's My job to grow her up in maturity. I've got this. It's your job to love her. Do that.* That's your word from the Lord. Let me get even more practical when it comes to the process. I recommend that you set aside thirty minutes each day to connect with the

Lord in a similar manner. If you're in the habit of meeting with the Lord daily, then it will become easier and easier for you to hear God. Let the lamp of God's light shine in for at least thirty minutes; if your days are like other people's, then you'll probably see a bunch of darkness for the rest of the day. That's how the world works. So the thirty minutes you spend with God each day is vital. When you need to hear God about a specific decision or direction you need to take, set aside even more time, at least an extra hour or two. And if it's a very important decision, then you might even go away and spend half a day or even a weekend with the Lord to really be able to hear Him and spend time with Him.

I never want anyone to be rigid about a time requirement. Meeting with the Lord isn't about crossing an item off your list, and it's important not to fulfill a specified amount of time as you would a duty roster. The point is that you deliberately choose to seek the presence and voice of the Lord. I believe that if you set aside thirty minutes a day to hear from God, then your life will slowly begin to change for the better. Later, after time has gone by and you need to make an important decision, you'll already be in the habit of hearing God. You'll already know how to come into His presence through praise. You'll already know how to write your prayers down and how to hear God through a story in the Bible or a specific verse.

That's what I want for you.

Your Word from the Lord Today

After my daughter, Elaine, graduated from high school, she went to junior college first, and we began to pray about her going to a university. A friend of mind, Dr. Mark Rutland, had just become the president of Oral Roberts University (ORU) in Tulsa, Oklahoma, and when I'd heard he'd become president, something just sort of leapt in my heart.

I knew Dr. Rutland to be a wise and compassionate man of God, and I knew the school would be in excellent hands under his leadership. In a week or two I was headed to Tulsa, where a local church had invited me to be guest speaker one Sunday. My wife, Debbie, and Elaine were set to come with me, so I suggested to my family that we take some time and tour ORU while there.

Before we left, I called Dr. Rutland's office, mentioned we were coming for a tour, and wondered aloud if Dr. Rutland had a few moments. If so, we'd love to spend a little time with him. It turned out he did, and so when we got there, it felt just as if God orchestrated our visit. Everything seemed so peaceful; it was wonderful. When we sat down with Dr. Rutland, he talked to Debbie and me for a bit at first, and then he turned to Elaine and started talking directly to her. His was a clear voice, a godly, father-figure type of voice, gentle but directional. Dr. Rutland asked Elaine what she was planning to do in the future, and how she was going to prepare for that, and what the Lord was calling her to do. After the conversation was over and we said our good-byes and left his office, Elaine turned to me, grinned, and said, "You know, it was just like God was talking to me through him."

We returned home to Dallas, and I asked Elaine if she'd had any more thoughts about the matter. And she said, "I really feel like I should go." We talked about her beginning her studies in midyear, in January, and I said, "Okay, Elaine, here's what you need to do now. You need to get a word from God." And her response was, "Oh, I thought you were going to do that for me."

That made me chuckle—only because I'd heard that line before. Not from Elaine but from people in my congregation. People approach me on a regular basis and ask me what God's word is for their lives, and I tell them flat out, "I have no idea. You have a personal relationship with God. God wants to talk to you personally. You ask Him."

I'm not trying to be snippy about that. There's a reason behind my directive. If the situation allows, I take them to two passages: Hebrews 4:16, where it says, "Let us therefore come boldly to the throne of grace, that we may obtain mercy and find grace to help in time of need," and to James 1:5, where it says, "If any of you lacks wisdom, let him ask of God, who gives to all liberally and without reproach, and it will be given to him." The key phrases in those passages show us that every believer can have confidence in approaching God ("come boldly"), and that God gives wisdom to *anyone* who asks Him. It's fine to ask godly leaders for counsel—and we'll talk more about that in chapters to come. But if you want a word from the Lord, then please don't depend on anyone hearing that word for you. It may happen in exceptional circumstances, as we'll look at in chapter 9, but it's not the norm. It's your responsibility and opportunity to seek the Lord yourself. God is your good and wise Father. And He loves it when His children approach Him.

So I encouraged Elaine to hear from the Lord herself. I explained that one big reason hearing from God was important was that once she got to school and a few months passed, then struggles and difficulties were bound to set in. Maybe she wouldn't like her roommate. Or she would have five long papers due and two big exams looming and a sore throat and the sniffles coming on. In those times of difficulty, the temptation would be for her to quit. But if she had a word from the Lord, then in those times of difficulty, she could look back on the word the Lord had given her at the start and know it was God's will for her to be there, difficulties and all.

So the next day she went to a lake (like father, like daughter), put on some worship music, and sought the presence of the Lord in prayer. After about three hours, she came back home and said, "Okay, God spoke to me. He wants me there." I asked her to explain.

Elaine took out her journal and showed me her notes. She said, "I was praying and writing things down, and these thoughts and Scripture references were coming to me, and, at first, I didn't know why they were coming. In prayer I'd written to God, 'It feels like You have an open door for me in Tulsa,' and I'd underlined *open door*. Then I wrote, 'I felt like Dr. Rutland was speaking right to me. I was surprised when he spoke to me because I thought he would just speak to my parents. But when he turned and spoke directly to me, it was so clear, like a trumpet's call, and I felt such a peace from God when Dr. Rutland spoke to me.' So I underlined *trumpet's call*."

I nodded, and then Elaine laughed when she recounted an earlier conversation I'd had with her. Whenever she'd talked about Tulsa, she'd been saying she was thinking of coming *down* to Tulsa. But from where we live in Texas, Oklahoma is due north. My daughter is blonde, and I didn't want anyone making blonde jokes about the girl I love, so I mentioned, in all correctness, that she should actually say come *up* to Tulsa. So she'd written that in her journal and had underlined *come up*.

Then she mentioned that one of her big concerns about going to university in the first place was what she'd do afterward. She could see herself going to school, but the future after that was unknown, and that was a big concern. So she'd written in her journal and prayed about that.

There was one more item: if she was going to go to school, she needed to be there on January 4. So she wrote that down and prayed about that. Then she looked at all the words she'd underlined in prayer: *open door, trumpet's call, come up, unknown future,* and *fourth*.

Elaine said, "As I was praying, the Holy Spirit impressed upon my heart a specific promise: *I am about to give you a revelation that on the fourth will be the first of many new things for you.* I wrote the promise in my journal too, and three words stuck out at me. I underlined those too: *revelation, fourth,* and *first*. And it was as if God said to me, *Okay, Elaine, that's your verse. Revelation 4:1.*"

So Elaine turned to Revelation 4:1, and this is what she read: "After these things I looked, and behold, a door standing open in heaven. And the first voice which I heard was like a trumpet speaking with me, saying, 'Come up here, and I will show you things which must take place after this.'"

Look at that verse again. That was her word from the Lord.

It's an open door.
As clear as a trumpet.
Come up here.
And I will show you the future.

This is the God we serve, a God who communicates with us in unique and sometimes even miraculous ways. All glory goes to Him. He is a speaking God, a relational God. He loves to guide and direct His children in good pathways. He invites us to run in the paths of His commands (Ps. 119:32 NIV), for He sets our hearts free. God's Word is a lamp for our feet and a light to our paths (v. 105), and He loves to speak to the hearts of His children.

God's direction is not always this clear and dramatic. But keep in mind Elaine was a young woman just beginning her independent experience with the Lord, and this was her first major life-changing decision. God clearly felt He needed to give her unmistakable direction. (By the way, she married a godly man named Ethan, who just happens to be—you guessed it—an ORU graduate.)

God will speak to you too.

Go to the Bible. Begin by worshipping Him and seeking His face. Listen for His voice. You can have confidence knowing that the Lord will speak.

CHAPTER FOUR

HEAR GOD'S VOICE
THROUGH WORSHIP

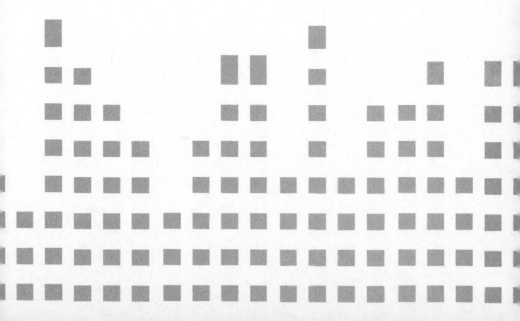

I will meet with you, and I will speak with you.

—Exodus 25:22

A friend of mine was leading worship at his church when a young man approached him afterward and asked if he could talk. The young man looked as though he had been crying.

"I finally get it," he said. "When we were worshipping, things finally made sense to me."

My friend asked him to explain.

The young man described how the congregation had been singing a particular worship song with a line from the chorus that repeated several times the theme of the goodness of God. This man and his wife had lost a baby to SIDS a year earlier, and they had been walking through much grief and pain. But when singing the song about God's goodness, he was struck anew with the mercy, peace, and love of God. His realization didn't make the pain all go away. But he knew that God was still good even though this extreme hardship had happened in their lives.

"It's hard to explain what exactly happened to me when we were singing that song," he said. "It's as if I wasn't just singing anymore. I felt that I was kneeling before God and seeing Him in all His glory. He knew everything about our baby girl, and He didn't give me a reason for her death. But somehow I didn't need to understand. Even without understanding, I knew that God was good, that He loves and cares for us. And I knew that my wife and I are somehow going to make it through this time. That's how things fit into perspective—when I was kneeling before a good God."

An Encounter with God

Friends, I want you to think about what happens during a worship service at your church. It doesn't matter if you attend on Sunday morning or Saturday evening or even if you watch a message online (although I would encourage everybody not to forsake the assembling of your-selves together and to actually attend church in person, being obedient to Hebrews 10:25).

At some churches the worship service feels like a list of items that need to be checked off: Welcome. Announcements. Songs. Offering. Sermon. Benediction. If that's the experience at your church, then I encourage you to carefully consider what's happening. I'm certainly not knocking well-planned services (we plan our services quite thoroughly at Gateway). But what I'm urging every believer to do is to make sure that you impose meaning on whatever you're doing in a worship service, all of it, always, every time.

Take, for instance, the singing time. See, the singing of songs is not merely the singing of songs. And the singing portion of a service is not merely the warm-up for the message. Rather, the singing of songs is actually a vehicle by which we can worship the Lord and connect with His person. We can enter into an awareness of His presence and com-mune with God. We can see God for who He truly is and then respond accordingly. We must never treat worshipping the Lord as merely a rote exercise. We must take this time seriously.

And please don't think that worship only happens at church. Worship can happen anytime. We might be driving in our car. We'll see a majestic sunset off in the distance, and just like that we're in prayer (with our eyes open if we're driving!) and singing songs of praise to God. Spontaneous times of worship can happen around a family dinner table. Worship can happen in a small-group experience at someone's house. Worship can happen when we're hiking alone in the wilderness or in the quietness of our hearts while lying in our beds at night just before sleep. Worship is an encounter with God. Anytime we see God for who He is and then respond accordingly—with or without music—that's worship.

Did you know that we can often hear God's voice best in worship?

God often speaks the loudest and clearest to us when we are worshipping Him. If you are seeking to hear from the Lord, then I encourage you to enter into a time of worship. Focus your heart and mind on the Lord and let Him speak to you.

Let's walk together through three things that happen when we worship God and see how it is that by worshipping Him we can better hear His voice.

1. During Worship God Meets with Us and Speaks with Us

I love the story in Exodus 25, where God met with the people of Israel. He instructed them to bring Him an offering and to build Him a tabernacle where He would dwell among them. It was no small task. God gave specific instructions on the size, shape, and furnishings of the tabernacle. It was to be overlaid with pure gold, inside and out. An elaborately decorated mercy seat (sort of like a special lid to a box) was to be placed on top of the ark. On this mercy seat, God's presence was manifested. Above the mercy seat, God said, "There I will meet with you, and I will speak with you" (Ex. 25:22).

Think about the two clauses of that verse. They are both so important. God is speaking, and He says,

> "I will meet with you,
>
> and
>
> I will speak with you."

Have you ever thought about how these two actions are closely related to each other, but they don't always happen at the same time? Many times in the Old Testament, God spoke to people through prophets, but He didn't always meet with the people when He did this. He essentially used a prophet as His messenger. Today you can speak with people via phone or Skype or e-mail and not meet with them. Back in

Genesis 28, God met with Jacob and spoke to him as he dreamed. When Jacob awoke, he remarked, "surely the LORD is in this place" (v. 16). Today you can meet with people or be in the same vicinity as people (like two strangers standing near each other on the subway) but never speak with them. Yet in the Exodus 25 passage, God says He both meets with people and speaks with them. How wonderful is that!

That's my prayer for all of us when we worship God—that God would both meet with us and speak with us—that we would truly have an encounter with God. See, God invites us to come to a place where we give Him all our fear, worries, anxiety, and stress. And in exchange we receive from Him love, joy, peace, goodness, meekness, faith, and self-control—the fruit of the Holy Spirit (Gal. 5:22). That's a really good exchange if you ask me. We come to a time of worship with fear in our hearts, and we leave with faith. We come with stress, and we leave with peace. This is part of the core and essence of worshipping God. In worship, we see God for who He truly is—a great God who loves us and who holds the universe in the palm of His hands. God is sovereign. He is in control. When we worship Him, He meets with us.

I love how the New International Version of the Bible translates Philippians 4:19, "My God will meet all your needs according to the riches of his glory in Christ Jesus." The word *meet* in the original Greek is *pleroo* and is sometimes translated "supply," as in "God will supply all your needs" (GNT).[1] But the word means more than simply filling up a container. It also has a personal component. The same word is used in Romans 15:13 (translated as "fill"), where Paul prays, "Now may the God of hope *fill* you with all joy and peace in believing, that you may abound in hope by the power of the Holy Spirit." The idea is that God meets with us personally. He supplies us by His own person what is lacking in us. He fills up our need by communing with us and transforming us. By the power of the Holy Spirit—a person—God causes us to abound in hope.

One of the other exciting things about Exodus 25:22 is that God doesn't say merely, "I want to speak *to* you." He says, "I want to speak *with* you." Do you see the difference? It's *with*, not simply *to*. This is a foundational idea. If someone merely speaks *to* you, then it's a one-way street. A professor in a classroom speaks to you. But the word *with* implies conversation. It's a two-way street where God wants to dialogue with us. He wants this personal aspect of communication to come through. It's as though God is saying, *I want you to talk with Me, and I will talk with you too. I want us to talk with each other.* That's good news for you and me. It means that we can converse with God in true dialogue about what's actually happening in our lives.

Some people might look at Exodus 25:22 and argue that this verse refers only to the Old Testament tabernacle, the one specifically used by the nation of Israel while they were out wandering in the wilderness. God will meet with His people and speak with them there. But what about nowadays? Wouldn't it be great if we still had the tabernacle?

There's more good news for us today. The tabernacle in the Old Testament was a literal tabernacle, yes; yet it was just a copy of the tabernacle to come, the tabernacle of our hearts. Second Corinthians 6:16 says, "For you are the temple of the living God. As God has said: 'I will dwell in them and walk among them. I will be their God, and they shall be My people.'" God does not simply dwell among us. He dwells within us. How? Christ dwells in our hearts through faith (Eph. 3:17).

2. During Worship We Gain Perspective

In times of worship, when we are truly meeting with God and God is speaking with us, that's where we gain perspective. It's where we see how big God is and how small we are, how good God is and how He takes away our iniquity.

Do you want joy? Do you want to be refreshed? Do you want perspective for life today? Psalm 16:11 says, "In Your presence is fullness of joy." Acts 3:19 describes how times of refreshing come from the presence of the Lord.

In the early 1990s, I was on staff at Shady Grove Church and doing well, but I was also tired. We had several intense ministry experiences and times of crisis around then, and I came to church one Sunday morning feeling exhausted and close to burnout. I was sitting in the congregation, and as we began to sing songs of worship, I prayed that God would show me a clear path forward. I asked Him to meet with me and speak with me. I longed for His presence and desperately wanted to hear His voice.

I know now that sometimes God puts a picture in our minds. Some people call this imagery. Some people call this seeing a vision. That's what happened that morning with me. It happened during an intense time of corporate worship. As we were "speaking to one another in psalms and hymns and spiritual songs, singing and making melody in [our] heart[s] to the Lord" (Eph. 5:19), I knelt down on the floor of the auditorium and saw a picture in my mind.

In my mind-picture I was at the entryway of a huge banquet hall, the very throne room of the Lord. At the far end of the room was a huge throne, and the Father was sitting on the throne. Other people were in the banqueting hall too, and they were joyfully feasting and worshipping the Lord together. But as I walked in, the Father asked everyone else to leave so it was just Him and me.

As I saw myself in this picture, I was dressed like a Roman soldier who'd just returned from a battle. I had a sword in my hand and wore a helmet on my head. I had cuts, and I was bleeding, dusty, and covered in grime and sweat. When everyone else left, I had a clear view of the Father.

"How is the battle going?" He asked.

"It's tough," I said. "But we're winning."

He set down His scepter, took the heavy crown off His head, and stood up. I set down my sword and took the helmet off my head. Then

He motioned me forward and opened His arms wide. I ran forward and jumped in His arms.

"Good to see you, son," He said.

"It's good to see You, too, Dad," I said.

And then He was sitting on His throne again, and I was still with the Father. But then I wasn't a tough grown-up soldier anymore. I was a child, a little boy, three or four years old, and I was sitting on my Daddy's lap, perfectly at rest, just as any little child would be with a good father. I still had scars, even then. But in His presence the scars were healing. He would run His fingers over the scars, and they would go away. I slept for a while on His lap and rested. Then I woke up. He kissed me on the forehead and said, "I'm so proud of you, son."

"Thank You, Dad," I said.

Then I was a grown man again, a soldier, and I put my helmet back on and picked up my sword. The doors to the banquet hall opened again, and all the people came back in. The Father held out His scepter to me and said, "Go in strength."

I held out my sword and walked out of the room.

The picture faded, and I was back in church again, back worshipping the Lord. I stood up—the same song was still being sung—and I felt refreshed and strong, ready to go back to the battle again. To me, that was the voice of the Lord. He was reminding me that in His presence I would find healing and refreshing. I might be a soldier on the battlefield, but in His presence I am His beloved son.

I don't have visions like that every Sunday. In fact, Debbie and I have had only a few visions like that in our entire lifetimes. And I'm not saying a vision is a normative experience for everybody who attends a worship service. But I'm saying that what I saw in my mind and heart during one particularly intense time of worship that day has given me strength even to this day.

In Isaiah 6:1–4, the prophet Isaiah describes a vision of his own. In the vision, Isaiah saw the Lord sitting on a throne, high and lifted up, and angels surrounded the Lord, crying to one another, "Holy, holy, holy is the LORD of hosts; the whole earth is full of His glory." Isaiah's spiritual eyes were opened, and he saw the Lord in all His sovereignty, in all His majesty. Isaiah saw the King of the universe—how He is over all, above all, higher than all, and greater than all. That point of truth is where worship begins for us too; it's when we see who God is, when we remember who it is that we serve, the God of all glory. And Isaiah responded accordingly. In Isaiah 6:5, he said, "Woe is me, for I am undone! Because I am a man of unclean lips, and I dwell in the midst of a people of unclean lips; for my eyes have seen the King, the LORD of hosts."

That's our invitation too—to see God for who He is. When we truly see how great He is, then we can easily see how small our problems are in light of Him. Nothing is too difficult for God. Nothing! When we see how holy God is, then we see our weaknesses and frailties in light of Him. We see our own sinfulness and how far short of His glory we fall. It's not a bad thing to see that. It can bring us to the Savior and usher us into the worship experience. Even though God is holy, He is able to inhabit our praises. John 3:16 is a famous Bible verse that describes so clearly our intense need for a savior: "For God so loved the world that He gave His only begotten Son, that whoever believes in Him should not perish but have everlasting life." That's clear—without God, we perish. With God, we have everlasting life.

In Isaiah 6:6–7, one of the angels flew to Isaiah with a live coal in his hands. The angel touched Isaiah's mouth with the live coal and said, "Behold, this has touched your lips; your iniquity is taken away, and your sin purged." That's a picture of God's grace. God does for us what we cannot do for ourselves. He takes a coal from the altar and cleanses us completely. Our iniquity is taken away. Our sins are removed "as far as the east is from the west" (Ps. 103:12).

With our sins taken care of, restoration and fellowship happen in God's presence. When we are in worship, we get our eyes off our problems, and we see how great He is. We see how wonderful, loving, kind, and forgiving He is, and we know we've been washed clean; our iniquity is taken away. With clean eyes, our whole outlook clears up, and we see things from God's perspective.

3. During Worship We Are Emboldened and Empowered

Debbie and I were in Guatemala a few years back on a mission trip. If you've never been on a short-term mission trip, then I highly encourage you to go. We had a free afternoon one day, so Juan Constantino (one of our pastors) and his wife and Debbie and I decided to go shopping.

I should point out that I did not make this decision myself. It was made for me. I've never been a fan of shopping. In fact, I'd say this even stronger: I absolutely hate shopping. My daughter, Elaine, loves it when I go shopping with her, and she often asks me to go, but I say, "Sugar, that's the one thing I hate to do. Drag me behind the car, but please don't take me shopping."

Anyway, we went. We were walking along in one of the shopping districts, and Juan and I were walking a few paces behind our wives. They were talking between themselves, but Juan and I were mostly quiet, taking in the sights and sounds and smells of the marketplace.

All of a sudden I found myself talking to the Lord, in a conversation wholly within myself. I was worshipping. I wasn't singing out loud, but I had a worship song in my mind, and I had a clear realization of the presence of God—even while out shopping. *God is with us. He's good. He's great. And He loves us.* That's what I was thinking. I was reminded of how the Lord wants to meet with us and speak with us.

God's voice spoke to my heart and said, *Robert, what do you hate to do more than anything on this earth?*

"Shopping," I said.

Right, God said. *And what do you love to do more than anything on this earth?*

"Connect people to You," I said in all sincerity. Evangelism is truly one of the things I love to do best. I love to connect people to God whether they're saved, lost, unchurched, or churched.

Okay, God said. *Then why don't you do that right now. While Debbie is shopping, doing this thing that she enjoys, why don't you do what you love to do at the same time?*

The very next shop we walked into, Christian music was playing. I walked up to the owner of the shop and asked, "Are you a Christian?" Juan interpreted for me.

"No, I'm not," the shop owner said.

"I'm curious why you're listening to Christian music," I said.

"Oh, simply because I like it," he said.

I'd never thought to ask this, but right then the Holy Spirit must have planted the right words in my mind because I asked, "Has anyone ever told you how easy it is to become a Christian?"

The shopkeeper's eyes lit up. "Easy? No. As a matter of fact, I've been told that it's very hard and that it takes a long time to become a Christian."

"That's not true," I said. I took out a Bible and showed him how to get saved. Five minutes later, right there in his store, he prayed to receive Christ into his heart. That's the voice of the Lord at work. About a year later I heard news of the man. He was totally on fire for God, worshipping and fellowshipping at a church near his shop.

What's so important about worship? God can speak to us when we worship. It's not just singing or checking items off a list. It can happen anywhere, anytime when we enter into His presence; we can see a fresh glimpse of God and hear His voice. Jesus is talking in Revelation 3:20 and says, "Behold, I stand at the door and knock. If anyone hears My voice and opens the door, I will come in to him and dine with him, and he with Me." This passage is not talking about food. It's talking about being in communion with God. The emphasis is on the One with whom we are dining.

When we worship the Lord, we look intently at Him, we listen to His voice, and we learn from Him. To look at God is an experience much the same as Moses had when he turned aside and drew near to the voice in the burning bush (Ex. 3:1–5). Moses set his gaze on the bush. He stopped what he was doing and focused on the Lord.

That's our invitation in worship as well. If we're sitting in church, there are always a million things we could be thinking of—maybe the news we heard on the radio on the drive to church, or the paper we need to write for school, or the carpool schedule for the upcoming week. A temptation always exists to let our minds wander. But Christ invites us to focus our thoughts and hearts on Him. This requires a deliberate action on our part. Purposefully, we set aside the thoughts of the world and set our minds on things above. Second Corinthians 3:18 says, "But we all, with unveiled face, beholding as in a mirror the glory of the Lord, are being transformed into the same image from glory to glory, just as by the Spirit of the Lord."

When we aim to listen to the Lord in worship, we can intentionally quiet our minds and hearts and incline our ears His direction. When my children were little, and I wanted to speak to them about something important, I always told my kids to look at me first. Once I had their full visual attention, it was amazing how much better they could hear me! God is the same way. He wants our full attention. Whenever we have our elder meetings at church, we long to hear from the Lord. So we spend the first portion of the meeting in worship and prayer. We always want to be deliberate about sitting in the presence of the Lord first. That way, we are much more inclined to listen to Him.

In God's presence we can learn from Him. Psalm 103:7 says, "He made known His ways to Moses, His acts to the children of Israel." God teaches us today as well. Jesus said in John 14:26, "But the Helper, the Holy Spirit, whom the Father will send in My name, He will teach you all things, and bring to your remembrance all things that I said to you."

I love how Psalm 73:1–17 describes the process of learning from the Lord:

> Truly God is good to Israel,
> To such as are pure in heart.
> But as for me, my feet had almost stumbled;
> My steps had nearly slipped.
> For I was envious of the boastful,
> When I saw the prosperity of the wicked.
>
> For there are no pangs in their death,
> But their strength is firm.
> They are not in trouble as other men,
> Nor are they plagued like other men.
> Therefore pride serves as their necklace;
> Violence covers them like a garment.
> Their eyes bulge with abundance;
> They have more than heart could wish.
> They scoff and speak wickedly concerning oppression;
> They speak loftily.
> They set their mouth against the heavens,
> And their tongue walks through the earth.
>
> Therefore his people return here,
> And waters of a full cup are drained by them.
> And they say, "How does God know?
> And is there knowledge in the Most High?"
> Behold, these are the ungodly,

Who are always at ease;
They increase in riches.
Surely I have cleansed my heart in vain,
And washed my hands in innocence.
For all day long I have been plagued,
And chastened every morning.

If I had said, "I will speak thus,"
Behold, I would have been untrue to the generation of Your
    children.
When I thought how to understand this,
It was too painful for me—
Until I went into the sanctuary of God;
Then I understood their end.

The psalmist begins his prayer by telling how he was in despair. He was envious of the boastful, jealous when he saw the prosperity of the wicked. His feet had almost stumbled, and his steps had nearly slipped. He was tempted by the thought that following God was a waste of time. "Surely I have cleansed my heart in vain" (v. 13), he lamented.

Then everything changed. Notice the word *until* in verse 17. He was thinking the wrong way and almost fell *until* he went into the sanctuary of God. His perspective changed when he went into the sanctuary of God and *met with* and *talked with* God. The rest of the psalm describes his changed perspective. He says in verses 23–26:

Nevertheless I am continually with You;
You hold me by my right hand.
You will guide me with Your counsel,
And afterward receive me to glory.

Whom have I in heaven but You?
And there is none upon earth that I desire besides You.
My flesh and my heart fail;
But God is the strength of my heart and my portion forever.

It was when he went into the sanctuary of the Lord that the writer's whole outlook shifted.

This is worship. It's a picture of a believer drawing near to God. The man has put his trust in God, and he worships Him. He is emboldened and empowered and ready to be led forth.

Move to Bethel

Right before we planted Gateway Church, Debbie and I felt led by the Lord to put our house up for sale and move closer to the area where Gateway was going to be located.

I must say, however, that we weren't optimistic initially about selling our house. The previous January, we'd put our house up for sale, and nobody had looked at it. Not a soul. It was priced right, the house showed well, we had a good real estate agent, and it was a buyer's market. In fact, three other houses in our neighborhood went on sale at the same time we put our house on the market, and all three sold within a month. But nobody came and looked at ours. So when we heard from the Lord about trying to sell our house again, Debbie and I were certainly willing to sell it, but I think we doubted our own ability to hear from the Lord.

We were sitting in church one Sunday right about that time and worshipping the Lord, and I felt a distinct impression to read Genesis 35:1—but to read it out of Debbie's Bible. That was strange. I knew what Genesis 35:1 said in my Bible. I opened it again and read the verse out of my New King James Version: "Then God said to Jacob, 'Arise, go up to Bethel and dwell there; and make an altar there to God.'"

God had impressed the verse on my heart earlier as a word about starting a church. He wanted me to go somewhere, dwell somewhere, and make an altar to the Lord there. Fine. I was doing that. But why did I feel this distinct nudge to read this verse out of Debbie's Bible? She was using the New Living Translation. I set down my Bible, opened hers, and read the verse again: "Then God said to Jacob, 'Get ready and move to Bethel and settle there. Build an altar there to . . . God.'"

Move to Bethel.

That was the changed word God wanted me to see. Not simply *dwell* there, but *move* there.

I laid down Debbie's Bible and continued to worship the Lord. As I worshipped, I felt another distinct impression—to list our house again and to do so quickly. When Debbie and I got home from church that day, we talked about and prayed through the decision. We discussed the verse the Lord had revealed to me in worship that day. The next day we put our house back up for sale. Within two weeks we had not just one buyer but two. A bidding war ensued over our house, and it sold soon after that. We were able to move to the area where we planted the church.

Friends, the singing of worship songs is not merely the singing of songs. And the singing portion of a service is not merely the warm-up for the message. Rather, the singing of songs and all the so-called preliminaries of a service (such as an offering or a Scripture reading) are actually vehicles by which we can worship the Lord. We can enter into His presence and commune with God. We can see God for who He is and then respond accordingly. We must take this time seriously. We can never think of worshipping the Lord as merely a rote exercise. Worship continues as we listen to a godly message from the Word of God. When our hearts' focus is right, we hear the message as God having a conversation with us. <u>Worship is an encounter with God</u>. Anytime we see God for who He is and then respond accordingly—that's worship.

We can often hear God's voice more clearly in worship. If you are seeking to hear from the Lord, then I encourage you to enter a time of worship. Quiet your heart, focus on the Lord, learn from Him, and let Him guide your paths.

CHAPTER FIVE

VALUE HIS VOICE

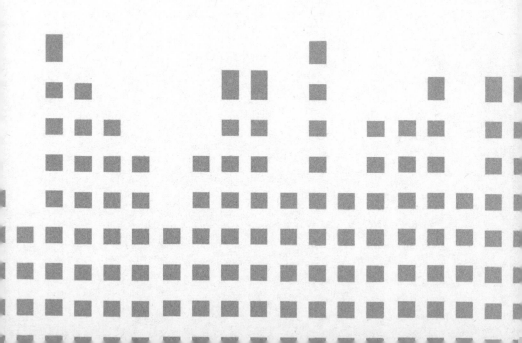

Be still, and know that I am God.
—Psalm 46:10

In a dream one night in 1993, God gave me a vision for ministry. It was a larger vision than I could have ever come up with on my own, and it was one of the most specific words from the Lord I'd ever received. God was speaking to me in the dream. This was His word to me: *I want you to build a church of thirty thousand people that reaches three hundred thousand in the Dallas–Fort Worth Metroplex. I also want this church to reach three million people in Texas, thirty million people in America, and three hundred million people around the world.*

Wow! I could hardly imagine a ministry with those kinds of numbers. The path forward seemed impossible—too hard, too steep. It wasn't even the idea of the large numbers that stunned me. I knew the large numbers were not the core of the vision—it was the changed hearts and lives that those numbers represented. Still, the vision felt too big, nothing I could possibly handle on my own. I wondered if maybe I had misunderstood the Lord.

But the very next morning I read 1 Samuel 11:8: "When he numbered them . . . the children of Israel were three hundred thousand, and the men of Judah thirty thousand." Immediately when I read those numbers, the Lord confirmed in my heart that the dream I'd had the night before had been from Him.

This is not the portion of Scripture where King David numbered the people of Israel in a census to show how much power he had apart from the Lord. (In that portion of Scripture, 1 Chronicles 21:1–7, King David was condemned for his act of numbering.) Rather, in the portion of Scripture I read, the ungodly nation of the Ammonites had come against the Israelites who lived in Jabesh Gilead and besieged them. The men of Jabesh Gilead pleaded for a treaty. Basically they said, "Don't make war on us, and we'll be your slaves," a proposal for an unholy treaty. The Ammonites agreed not to make war on Jabesh Gilead if all the men of the city would submit to having their right eyes gouged out to disgrace and weaken the whole nation.

The leaders of Jabesh Gilead stalled the enemy; meanwhile, the Spirit of the Lord came upon King Saul to launch a rescue. The people of Israel and Judah were numbered to show their solidarity and strength before the Lord.

It was a holy act of numbering.

See, I was in the process of learning to value the voice of the Lord. I would have told you I valued His voice already, but God wanted me to learn this lesson more than once. He wanted me to learn it, and learn it, and learn it again. Why? That's often what it takes with us.

In Mark 6:30–44, Jesus did one miracle and His disciples saw it—He fed five thousand people using only five loaves of bread and two small fish. Then right after that, in Mark 6:45–56, Jesus miraculously calmed the storm for His disciples—and notice their response: *Wow—you can do that too?* "Then [Jesus] climbed into the boat with them, and the wind died down. They were completely amazed, *for they had not understood about the loaves*; their hearts were hardened" (Mark 6:51–52 NIV).

The same can often be true of us when we're seeking a word from the Lord. We learn to value His voice only over time. We must hear Him again and again and again.

Stepping Out in Faith

At first, I didn't know what to do with the vision.

At the time the dream came to me, I was on staff at Shady Grove Church, and Pastor Olen Griffing, the founding senior pastor, had been talking to me about being a senior pastor one day. I sensed that the

Lord was telling me to wait, to stay where I was for the time being, and the vision would play out as the Lord arranged things in the future. That was fine with me. The Lord could move any way He wanted. He would show me when to begin and how. A year passed, and another and another. When seven years had finally passed, I went to the Prayer Center at the church to spend a day with the Lord, and He renewed the vision again and started speaking to me about planting a church in the Dallas–Fort Worth Metroplex, northwest of Shady Grove.

Only then did I share with Pastor Olen what the Lord had spoken to me. I knew I needed to resign from Shady Grove to progress forward with the vision. He was disappointed to see me leave, but he knew the transition was from the Lord. Pastor Olen and the elders gave me their blessing and said they thought it would be a good idea if, once I resigned, I traveled and rested for an undisclosed amount of time before planting a church. So they graciously gave me a two-month sabbatical with pay. I wasn't sure how long of a break the Lord wanted me to take, or what my family would do for finances after those two months were up, but I knew the Lord would lead and provide.

Later that same day I resigned, and I called my friend Pastor Jimmy Evans to let him know I was taking a break and traveling for a while. I told him I wasn't jumping into a new church plant right away and was available if he needed me to come speak. Pastor Jimmy immediately said, "I want you to travel and speak to our Trinity Fellowship Association of Churches [about seventy churches]. Whatever Shady Grove has been paying you, I'll pay you the same." I had resigned not knowing where my next paycheck was going to come from, but within a few hours I'd been hired by Trinity Fellowship Church at the exact same salary.

I obeyed the Lord's leading and stepped out in faith, and God immediately provided. It's as though I had taken a step forward, but my back foot had left the ground before my front foot had landed. Yet when

I landed, I was safe because of Jesus. To me, landing safely was another confirmation that the Lord was in this.

What's in a Name?

When the time came to begin the new work, I was wondering in prayer about what we should name our new church. I knew that a name is important. One morning in my quiet time, the Lord impressed upon my heart the name Gateway. A few days later I came across the twenty-eighth chapter of Genesis. It records that Jacob had a dream where he saw heaven open up and angels ascending and descending between heaven and earth. In this dream, Jacob had an encounter with God Himself in which God made a remarkable promise to him. When Jacob woke up, he exclaimed, "Surely the LORD is in this place. . . . What an awesome place this is! It is none other than the house of God, the very gateway to heaven!" (Gen. 28:16–17 NLT). That one phrase leapt out at me—*the very gateway to heaven.*

That was exactly what I wanted for Gateway Church. I wanted it to be a place where people encountered the presence of God; where people who had never experienced the love, power, and peace of God would feel His presence the moment they walked in the door, and they would declare, "Surely the Lord is in this place!"

I had been feeling that the Southlake region of Dallas–Fort Worth was the place we were to begin the church, and soon after this feeling began, Debbie and I drove out there to have dinner with some friends. Just as we were taking the exit onto Southlake Boulevard, I said to her, "I feel like the Lord gave me the name of the church."

"Oh! What is it?" she asked.

"Gateway," I said.

Right at that moment we saw a huge sign that said, "Coming soon! Gateway Shopping Plaza." (This is the same shopping plaza that's in that location today, but it hadn't been built then. There was only a sign.) We just laughed.

We picked up our friends, and I began telling them about the name and seeing the sign. We drove back to show them the sign, but here's the remarkable thing: when we looked over to see it, there was no sign. We were driving in a different direction on the freeway then, so we thought maybe we couldn't see it from that angle. After we ate, we drove back and took the exact same exit as we had the first time. As we turned left to drive over the bridge, I said, "Look; you'll be able to see it really well." But there was no sign. We never saw that sign again.

Was the sign a vision that the Lord had given Debbie and me both for a moment? Or did we see a substantial post-and-plywood sign that had subsequently fallen down or been carted away for some reason? We would never know. But what we did know is that the Lord had used an image of a sign in His mysterious way to speak to us in confirmation of the thoughts He had given me earlier.

God's Voice and the Timing of Our First Service

God was equally vocal and specific about the timing of our first service. In the early months of 2000, Debbie and I were praying about when we should have our first service. One day I was reading a book in one part of the house, and Debbie was reading a different book in another part of the house. In the book she was reading, there was a story about a church that had its first service on Easter. Instantly, the Lord spoke to her and said, *Gateway's first service should be on Easter.* In the book I was reading, a pastor was praying for revival, and the Lord told him, *I'm going to send revival to the church on Easter.* At that moment the Lord spoke to my heart, saying, *Start on Easter.*

I went into the other room and said to Debbie, "I know when we're supposed to start the church. The Lord just spoke to me."

And she said, "Well, the Lord just told me too."

"What did He tell you?"

"Easter," she said.

And, of course, I agreed, "Easter."

Right after that I was talking to Pastor Jimmy on the phone, and I told him the Lord had given us the date we were to start the church. And he said, "Well, I know when you're supposed to start the church because He told me too."

"Well, what did He tell you?" I asked.

"Easter."

A short time later Pastor Wayne Drain and I were leading a meeting together. The subject that day was how a prophetic ministry is still vital and needed today in the church. Pastor Wayne asked a man to stand up and began to give the man a word from the Lord, then suddenly stopped, turned around, and said, "Robert, the Lord says, 'Easter, Easter, Easter.'" And he turned right back around and kept giving the word to the man.

These confirmations proved what the Bible says: "'By the mouth of two or three witnesses every word may be established'" (Matt. 18:16; 2 Cor. 13:1).

There was no dispute. Easter Sunday, April 23, 2000, would be Gateway's first service.

Additional Confirmation

Three months after we planted Gateway Church, during my quiet time, I was using a plan where I was reading through the Bible in a year. I had forgotten about the scripture the Lord had used to confirm the dream He'd given me seven years earlier until I got to 1 Samuel 11. I read those words again: "When he numbered them . . . the children of Israel were three hundred thousand, and the men of Judah thirty thousand" (v. 8). The Lord said to me, *I'm going to remind you what I've called you to do. I'm going to confirm these numbers to you again.* I remembered that when we'd planted the church, Trinity Fellowship (where Jimmy Evans was the senior pastor at the time) had given us thirty thousand dollars in seed money to start.

Later that same day I had lunch with a man who had visited our church twice, and at the end of the lunch he said, "My family and I are going to join the church, and we're excited about it! Every now and then, we have some resources we can sow into the kingdom. The Lord has put a specific amount on my heart, and I want to give this to the church." He handed me a check and said, "He told me to tell you this amount is going to confirm something to you."

I thanked the man and told him how grateful we were. We said good-bye, and after I got in my car, I reached into my pocket and pulled out the check—it was for three hundred thousand dollars. The Lord had confirmed both numbers that He had given me in a dream seven years before!

There's no doubt in my mind those numbers were from God. When He wants to do something, our part is to passionately serve Him with all our hearts. It's up to God to accomplish His Word; it's up to us to obey in faith. I knew God was telling me that if I would take care of the depth of my relationship with Him—by having a personal, daily, intimate, thriving relationship with Jesus Christ—then He would take care of the width of the ministry.

A Straightforward Blueprint

As I write this book, Gateway Church has been in existence for fifteen years. The numbers from the vision are only now becoming a reality, although we haven't hit them all yet, and there is more work to be done. What it says to us is that God has a long life and ministry ahead for us. We average about thirty thousand people attending weekly services at our campuses. Our services are videotaped and shown on seven different TV networks, sixteen times a week. Members of our worship team write many of our own worship songs, and they have gone all over the world, as do the books I write. So it's difficult to know exactly how many people we are reaching. A few years back, Debbie and I went on a ministry trip to London, Israel, and Egypt, and people in all three countries came up to us and said, "We watch your program on TV."

Why did I tell you this story? Numbers don't drive me. What drives me is my love for the Lord, my desire that my relationship with Him stays passionate, and my trust in His sovereignty that the real work of ministry comes from Him. I simply want to be a light for the kingdom of God and to live a life that's honoring to God.

I tell you this story to show one way over time that I learned to value God's voice. It's not that I didn't value His voice before. But I needed to learn—and then relearn over time—to recognize His voice and then rely upon Him all the more. The vision for planting Gateway Church didn't come from me. It came from God. There was no way I could implement that sort of plan. But God could. He's in control. I need to do my part in that and act as He leads me. Yet He is always the one in charge.

So how does this all relate to you? It's my prayer that you will learn to value God's voice in your own life as well.

I mentioned earlier how we talk about God's general will and God's specific will. When we have a job change or we're buying a new home or we have an important decision to make concerning our marriage or family or future, we want a specific word from the Lord. And we need one from Him too. And He will give us one. But my concern is that we sometimes try to hear a specific word from God without first developing the habit of hearing a general word from God every day. That's an important part of the process of learning to value God's voice.

If we just check in with God every six months or so whenever a big decision comes up, then we will miss out not only on knowing God's general will but also on a close, everyday friendship with God. So we must learn to value His voice, His general voice, on a regular basis if we want to hear His specific voice from time to time. If we're not in the habit of meeting with Him and hearing from Him on a regular basis, then it will be much more difficult to hear a specific word from God.

So how do we hear this general word of God? Let me offer four practical steps.

1. Set an Appointment with God

Let me ask you simply and directly: How much time in your daily schedule have you allotted to hearing God's voice? Many of us falsely believe we are too busy to make this a priority. But here's a practical recommendation: if you want to hear God, then set an appointment with God every day. Schedule God in.

Maybe that sounds heretical to you. To schedule a person into your life feels as if you are saying that you are the center of importance. You call the shots, and the other person's schedule revolves around yours. You certainly wouldn't schedule your wife into your life this way. Or your kids. Would you?

I challenge you to think about scheduling a different way. You arrange your schedule around what's most important. If something is important, then you make it a priority. You schedule your most important meetings. You schedule phone calls you don't want to miss. You schedule time for a vacation so you can get recharged. You schedule time with your doctor, dentist, attorney, or CPA. In this sense, scheduling doesn't denigrate the person of God in your life. It prioritizes Him.

In Exodus 19:10–11, we read about people setting an appointment with God: "Then the LORD said to Moses, 'Go to the people and consecrate them today and tomorrow, and let them wash their clothes. And let them be ready for the third day. For on the third day the LORD will come down upon Mount Sinai in the sight of all the people.'"

Notice what God is doing. He's setting an appointment to meet with the Israelites. God wants the people to be ready for His appointment. God comes to a prepared people in a prepared atmosphere. What's important about this story in the Bible is that God didn't simply say to Moses, "Hey, gather everybody around any old time." He basically said, "Get them ready. In three days, let them hear the word of the Lord." Exodus 19:19 continues the story: "And when the blast of the trumpet sounded long and became louder and louder, Moses spoke, and God answered him by voice."

When you look through the Bible at the times people had encounters with God, there often was some preparation beforehand. Just think of all the preparation that happens at a church before Sunday. What would happen if you came one weekend and no one greeted you when you came in because there were no greeters? Then you went to drop your children off at a Sunday school class, but there were no teachers at the children's classes—the lights weren't even on. Then you came into the sanctuary, but no chairs were set up. The worship team hadn't rehearsed. No one had even picked out any songs to sing. No one was qualified to run a soundboard, and the PA system hadn't even been turned on. There were no ushers to help you find a seat. No one handed you a bulletin. The pastor hadn't prepared any sermon notes. He just stood up and said, "Well, aw shucks, I guess I should say something, so here I go."

Yes, I am aware of churches that put little preparation into the weekend services, and then they blame low attendance, apathetic congregants, lack of discipleship, few returning guests, and a shoddy worship experience on other things. Certainly the Holy Spirit can work at any time and any place, and certainly we want to allow for the Holy Spirit to move any way He wants during a weekend service. But the Holy Spirit is never disorganized. In fact, the Holy Spirit often works best through prepared soil. The Holy Spirit can certainly speak on a Tuesday to a leader about what He wants to do the following Sunday so that a well-prepared service is also a Spirit-led service.

Even for churches that are more informal in style, God still advocates preparation and order, not chaos and disorder. Paul says in 1 Corinthians

14:26 and 33, "How is it then, brethren? Whenever you come together, each of you has a psalm, has a teaching, has a tongue, has a revelation, has an interpretation. Let all things be done for edification. . . . For God is not the author of confusion but of peace, as in all the churches of the saints." That's a picture of organization, even informal organization. Everyone is prepared and orderly.

The same is true when we want to hear the voice of God. We are invited to prepare the ground first for planting, and one of the best ways we can do this is to set an appointment. If we don't set an appointment to meet with God, then we'll miss our time with Him. You ask, how can you miss it if you don't set it in the first place? My point exactly. The appointment isn't there. Without an appointment, the day tends to dribble away on other things.

Some Christians insist that the only time to set an appointment with God is early in the morning, preferably the earlier the better. I'd say that 5:00 a.m. might be the best time for some people, but not everybody will be at his or her best at 5:00 a.m. So pick your best time. It's far more important that we have time with God than when that time is set; that is, the time factor is secondary to the actual appointment. If you're a morning person, set a morning appointment. Some people will choose to meet with God on their lunch hour. They'll take their lunches and their Bibles and get away to a park bench and meet with Him there. If you're a parent of small children, your best time might be after you get them all in bed in the evening and the house finally grows quiet.

I also recommend finding consistent places of sanctuary where you can meet with the Lord. This might be a room in your house or a coffee shop down the street or a park that overlooks a lake. You might have more than one place, and that's fine. A place of sanctuary, in this sense, is wherever you can meet with the Lord and be focused and uninterrupted. It's a place of solitude for you and God, even though it might be in a public place. Our lead executive senior pastor, Tom Lane, takes his journal and Bible and meets with God every morning at McDonald's. He's done that for more than thirty years, and it works well for him.

So set an appointment and meet with God. What happens first during this meeting?

2. Be Still and Worship

The appointment begins as we are still before Him. And we worship Him.

Being still is hard for many of us, yet the Bible exhorts us, "Be still, and know that I am God" (Ps. 46:10). The New American Standard Bible words it this way, "Cease striving and know that I am God." In either translation, the wording reflects a posture of quietness before the Lord—of listening, of faithful expectancy, of casting cares and anxiety at God's feet because He cares for us (1 Peter 5:7; Ps. 55:22).

We see this posture of being still throughout Scripture. As soon as the Israelites first left their bondage in Egypt, Pharaoh changed his mind about letting them go. He jumped into his chariot and took his army with him, chasing the Israelites all the way to the Red Sea. As Pharaoh approached, the Israelites saw a vast army bearing down on them. The Israelites couldn't progress forward because the sea blocked their path. They started to lament that it would have been better off for them to stay in Egypt as slaves. But they would find out that they didn't need to fight this battle: "Moses answered the people, 'Do not be afraid. Stand firm and you will see the deliverance the LORD will bring you today. The Egyptians you see today you will never see again. The LORD will fight for you; you need only to be still'" (Ex. 14:13–14 NIV).

Did you catch the commands?

"Stand firm . . .
see the deliverance the LORD will bring you . . .
. . . you need only to be still."

I love the story in 2 Chronicles 20 where three armies had surrounded Judah and Jerusalem. The people were terrified, and there, with enemies all around them, they stood before the Lord, wondering what to do. Then the Spirit of the Lord came on a man named Jahaziel, a Levite, and he stood in the assembly and said, "Do not be afraid or discouraged because of this vast army. For the battle is not yours, but God's. . . . You will not have to fight this battle. Take up your positions; stand firm and see the deliverance the LORD will give you" (vv. 15, 17 NIV).

Note the actions the Israelites take:

And when [the king] had consulted with the people, he appointed those who should sing to the LORD, and who should praise the beauty of holiness, as they went out before the army and were saying:

"Praise the LORD,
For His mercy endures forever."

Now when they began to sing and to praise, the LORD set ambushes against the people of Ammon, Moab, and Mount Seir, who had come against Judah; and they were defeated. For the people of Ammon and Moab stood up against the inhabitants of Mount Seir to utterly kill and destroy them. And when they had made an end of the inhabitants of Seir, they helped to destroy one another.

So when Judah came to a place overlooking the wilderness, they looked toward the multitude; and there were their dead bodies, fallen on the earth. No one had escaped. (2 Chronicles 20:21–24)

If you ask me, I'd say that's a pretty good way to win a war! Tell the musicians to go out first. They'll lead everybody in singing and worshipping God, and then God will take care of the rest.

The pattern is described again in Acts 13:2: "While they were worshiping the Lord and fasting, the Holy Spirit said, 'Set apart for me Barnabas and Saul for the work to which I have called them'" (NIV). Notice the sequence of the actions in that verse. Worshipping came first. The Holy Spirit's speaking came second.

Every one of us fights battles. Maybe you're fighting a battle in your health, or in your family, or in your job, or in your marriage, or for your future. The pattern is this: first, stand still before God and worship Him; second, the Holy Spirit will show you what to do.

What specifically might standing still and worshipping look like? For me, it means going away to a quiet place where I can put aside the thoughts of the day. I turn on some worship music and literally start singing. Sometimes I don't use music. I just sing. Often I ask God first, "Lord, what song do You want me to sing to you today?" And the Lord will bring a worship song to mind. I usually sing on the inside only because when I sing on the outside, people cry and animals howl. It's not a pretty sight. The point is that my heart is in line with God's heart through the purposeful and strategic act of worship.

So I set an appointment to meet with God, then purposely quiet my heart, and then worship the Lord. After that comes the amazing Creator-creature dialogue we call praying and reading.

3. Pray and Read

Mark 1:35 sets the pattern: "Now in the morning, having risen a long while before daylight, [Jesus] went out and departed to a solitary place; and there He prayed." Psalms 119:147 says, "I rise before the dawning of the morning, and cry for help; I hope in Your word."

When we pray like this, what do we pray for? We pray for whatever is on our hearts. We don't need to pray for the president of the United States every day unless the president is on our hearts. We don't need to pray for our church that day unless our church is on our hearts. Just talk to God, and then read the Bible. Where? The best answer is on the inside. Second Timothy 3:16–17 reminds us, "All Scripture is given by inspiration of God, and is profitable for doctrine, for reproof, for correction, for instruction in righteousness, that the man of God may be complete, thoroughly equipped for every good work."

Look again at the first word of that verse—*all*. People ask me what *all* means, and I clear my throat and say, "Well, in the original Greek, *all* means . . . uh . . . *all*." That means everything in the Bible is useful. *Everything.* Read from the Gospels. Read the book of Acts. Read from Ruth or Hosea or 1 Peter or the Psalms. Start in Genesis. Start in Matthew. Start in Jude. Read one chapter of Proverbs every day for a month. It doesn't matter where you read from in the Bible. It's all useful.

So I set an appointment and then become still and worship the Lord. Then I read and pray. Then I listen and write.

4. Listen and Write

Listening to God is one of the hardest things for us to do. But if we learn to listen, then we will learn to hear God's voice. I say listen and write because one of the best ways I've learned to hear the voice of God is to write down thoughts and prayers when I meet with Him. The act of writing helps keep my mind focused, and it also helps me discern which verses apply to my specific situation.

Write down what you believe from Scripture are God's answers to your prayers. The discipline of writing also helps when you look back and see how God has directed your life over time.

Note this verse that comes from *The Message*: "My heart bursts its banks, spilling beauty and goodness. I pour it out in a poem to the king, shaping the river into words" (Ps. 45:1). The psalmist is talking about his time spent meeting with God. Here's what he's saying: "When I meet with God, my heart just seems to overflow, and the best thing that I can do is just write it in a poem."

In 1 Chronicles 28:19, David is referring to the intricate attention to detail needed to build the temple of God. "'All this,' said David, 'the LORD made me understand in writing, by His hand upon me, all the works of these plans.'" Here's what David was saying: "Whenever I met with God, God would speak to me about things regarding His temple. I would write things down, and as I wrote them, I would understand what God was saying."

The prophet Habakkuk describes the act of writing down a word from the Lord: "Then the LORD answered me and said: 'Write the vision and make it plain on tablets, that he may run who reads it'" (Hab. 2:2).

So set an appointment. Be still. Worship the Lord. Read and pray. Listen and write. You will not be writing inspired words, as the writers of the Bible were doing, but you will be writing your personal application of inspired Scripture, following the pattern of action set by Bible writers.

How to Catch a Lot of Fish

I mentioned that my son James has always been an avid fisherman, ever since he was a young boy. He's in his thirties today and busy with responsibilities at work and in family life. Yet when he was a boy, he was always watching TV shows about fishing, always reading books about fishing techniques, and always out fishing any chance he could get.

One time we went to Colorado on a family vacation. A trout pond was nearby. James was eleven or twelve, and he wanted to fish that pond something fierce. First, he went to the pond, walked around it, and studied the area, and then he went to the local store and selected the bait he wanted. But when he took the bait to the counter to pay for it, the shopkeeper said, "Son, I'm sorry, but that bait won't catch fish around here. The trout won't touch that kind of bait." I looked at my son, and he gave me a little nod, as if he knew what he was doing and wanted this bait anyway. So I let him do what he thought was best. He was the fishing expert. I wasn't. He purchased the bait.

James went back to the pond. One side of the pond was already thick with fishermen, but James walked around to the other side of the pond to where no fishermen were. He baited his hook, threw his line in the water, and started catching fish, one right after another.

Half an hour went by, and then an hour, and a funny thing started happening. One by one, all of these grown men on the other side of the pond started asking James questions about what he was using. Slowly, they inched their way around the pond so they could fish closer to where he was fishing. Pretty soon, the whole crowd had moved to his side.

What's the point? *Generally* James knew how to fish really well. He studied fishing all the time, even when he wasn't specifically trying to catch a fish. So when he *specifically* wanted to catch a fish, he knew exactly what he was doing, and he was able to catch many.

Hearing God's voice is like that. Every day we need to spend time in God's presence so we hear God's general voice. When we learn how to discern the general will of God on a regular basis, we are ready to hear God's specific word. God comes to a prepared atmosphere. As we make and keep appointments to meet with God, we'll learn to hear His voice.

Do you value God's voice? Do you value it so much that you regularly take time to hear Him? It's important for us to set regular appointments to be with God in order to learn from His Word and to hear His voice. We may struggle to hear and recognize the specific word of the Lord for our lives if we don't learn to seek and value the general word of the Lord through regular appointments with Him.

To develop a regular time with the Lord, set an appointment, be still and worship Him, pray, and read the Bible. Write down your prayers. Listen for His response.

Jeremiah 29:13 holds out a wonderful promise to us. God is talking and He says, "You will seek Me and find Me, when you search for Me with all your heart."

CHAPTER SIX

CALL FOR CONFIRMATION

"If now I have found favor in Your sight, then show
me a sign that it is You who talk with me."
—Judges 6:17

While on a mission trip in eastern Europe, I sensed the Lord leading us to minister in the country that was then called Yugoslavia. It was during their war for independence, more than twenty years ago now, and we were told it wasn't safe to travel to this country. But we sensed the Holy Spirit leading us to go there anyway and minister to the Christians and to the churches there.

We couldn't fly into the country; we could only drive. We weren't able to obtain visas, which meant we had no official notice of safe passage with us, and we were pretty sure the officials wouldn't let us in. But we were praying and decided to try anyway.

We arrived at the border in a car, and the guard stopped us. One of the men who drove us, a Yugoslavian national, had an association with the Red Cross. He flashed his Red Cross badge, and the guard took one look at the badge and whisked us right through. Who knew the Red Cross could be so powerful? We sensed our easy entry was from the Lord.

About two miles in from the border was a heavily guarded checkpoint that we also needed to cross. There, a guard stopped us and barked a bunch of orders to our driver in Slavic. I didn't know what he was saying, but I understood enough to know that he wanted our papers. This crossing wasn't going to be as easy. I had no papers.

Two other Yugoslavian nationals were with us in the car, and both men pulled out their documents immediately. The guard went to the first man and checked his papers, then walked around to the other man and checked his. I was next. I could feel my heart pounding in my chest, and all this while I kept praying the words of Zechariah 4:6, *O Lord Jesus, "'not by might nor by power, but by [Your] Spirit,' says the* LORD *of hosts."*

A few seconds before the guard got to me, a pretty girl pedaled by on a bicycle, stopped, and started talking to another guard just up the road from us. I'm telling you—God has a sense of humor, even in our most desperate times. The guard who was checking us took one look at the pretty girl, did a double take, and sort of mumbled something quickly, distracted, as if he wanted us all to hurry up so he could walk up the road and talk to the pretty girl himself. He was still looking up the road at the girl when he came to me and said, "Papers."

I didn't move.

Neither did the guard. But the driver of our car quickly said a bunch of words in Slavic and then said, "Dallas"—one word in English. It struck me as odd. I think he was saying I was from Dallas, but he could have said I was from the United States, or America, or even Texas. But he distinctly used the name of the city—Dallas.

The guard, still distracted by the pretty girl, glanced my direction and said in English, "Oh, Dallas Cowboys. Number one."

And I said, "Yes! Dallas Cowboys! You like the Dallas Cowboys?"

This time the guard looked at me more closely and grinned widely. Without asking to look at my papers, he motioned with his head and said, "Go ahead." Just like that—and off we drove. Praise the Lord for football!

You'd think that when God does such an overt work on our behalf, we'd no longer struggle to trust Him. This particular work of God turned out to be even more amazing than I'd understood at first. A while later in the car, the men and I were discussing the ins and outs of what it meant to cross the border as we had done. Initially I thought we'd simply crossed the borders without visas, something rare, but something permissible. But it turned out to be quite a bit more complicated than that. One of the men explained that we'd crossed the border without registering me, and that what we'd done was actually an unlawful offense. The year before, they had tried the same thing with a different pastor. He had been caught by the authorities and ended up going to prison in Yugoslavia for six months.

I gulped.

God had done amazingly above what we could ask or think and even what I could understand, and my heart praised Him. But why was I delivered and not that pastor a year ago? Why deliverance for one and not the other? We don't know, but we trust God is sovereign.

It was Friday night, and we finally arrived at our destination. We were based about thirty minutes away from the fighting but could actually hear gunfire and explosions going off nearby. I was staying in the home of a Yugoslavian pastor, and he offered me the best he had to sleep on—a tiny cot in his living room. He left to sleep elsewhere, and I was left alone in the room, and I started to take stock of where I was and what I was doing. Already, I'd been out of the States for two weeks. The trip was to last another week, and I felt a long way from home. I was able to get a phone call through to Debbie, and it was encouraging to hear her voice, but she was having a rough time of it too. One of our children was sick. Debbie didn't know what was wrong and intended to take him to the doctor. She was worried, and when I got off the phone with her, I felt worried too. I tried to sleep but couldn't. I knew the next two days were filled with meetings in the churches, and I kept expecting the authorities would catch me and throw me in jail for six months. I felt exhausted, overwhelmed, and frightened.

I didn't know what to do, so I got up, walked outside, and started to pray. I poured out my heart to God:

> Lord Jesus, I need to hear Your voice. If You truly want me
> on this trip, please let me know again. You've got to speak

to me because I can't handle this. Did You really want us to come to Yugoslavia? Please confirm to me that You did.

Still in prayer I opened my eyes and looked up into the night sky. It was a clear, crisp night, and I saw the Big Dipper and the North Star, the same stars in Yugoslavia that I could see in my backyard. Verses started coming to mind. "By the word of the LORD the heavens were made, their starry host by the breath of his mouth" (Ps. 33:6 NIV). "If I rise on the wings of the dawn, if I settle on the far side of the sea, even there your hand will guide me, your right hand will hold me fast" (139:9–10 NIV).

And God spoke to my heart and said, *Robert, I hold these stars in place. I'm holding your family in place, and I'm holding you in place.*

The peace of God came over me, comforting, reassuring. I went back into the house, lay down on that cot in the living room, and immediately fell fast asleep.

More than twenty years later I saw the same pastor who had hosted us on that trip. He said that our ministry had helped change the whole atmosphere of the churches in that region, and that influence had spread across the believers throughout the country. The glory isn't ours. All glory goes to God. He called. We responded to His voice.

I mentioned at the start of this book that the number one question I get asked as a pastor is "How can I hear the voice of God?" Well, I get asked an additional question about the number one question, and it's this: "How do I know if it is really God?" In other words, how do I know if God is truly speaking, and I'm not making up something in my mind? Is it okay to ask God to confirm His word?

The simple answer to that is yes—just as I had done when I looked up at the Yugoslavian night sky and asked God to confirm He'd spoken to us about the trip in the first place. It's okay because God always confirms His word. Let me repeat that:

God *always* confirms His word.

It's Okay to Seek Confirmation

Does that seem like a bold statement to you—that God always confirms His word? How do we know for sure? Let's look at a few scriptures that show how much the Holy Spirit values confirmation:

- Mark 16:20: "And they went out and preached everywhere, the Lord working with them and confirming the word through the accompanying signs."

  Here the teaching is plain: God confirmed the workings of Jesus and the disciples through miracles.
- Matthew 18:16: "But if he will not hear, take with you one or two more, that 'by the mouth of two or three witnesses every word may be established.'"

  Jesus gave this teaching in the context of dealing with a brother who sins against you. You are to go to the brother by yourself and tell him what he did was wrong. If he listens to you, you've helped restore fellowship. But if he refuses to listen, you're to take one or two people with you. Then, more than one person will be able to confirm the story and tell all that happened. The point here is that God understands and endorses the power of confirmation.
- 2 Corinthians 13:1: "This will be the third time I am coming to you. 'By the mouth of two or three witnesses every word shall be established.'"

  Paul is actually referring to the epistle he just wrote. Again, the point here is that the Holy Spirit values confirmation.

The story of Gideon's fleece in Judges 6 is perhaps the best-known Bible story that relates to confirmation. We've touched on this scripture before, but let's take a deeper look at it. The funny thing is that when we talk about Gideon, everybody seems to know about the most famous part of the story—the fleece. There are people who don't even know the Bible who talk about Gideon's fleece. But did you know there were several other times that Gideon asked God to confirm His word? These incidences happened in addition to the fleece.

As the story begins, the Israelites were being oppressed because of the Midianites, and they cried out to the Lord for relief. The Lord heard their prayers and appeared to a man named Gideon while he threshed wheat in a winepress. Back in those days a winepress was sort of a big stone hole in the ground. Can you picture the process of threshing wheat by hand? You toss it in the air and hope the wind will blow the chaff away, leaving only the kernels behind. Threshing is a heavy, dusty, messy business, particularly in the closed quarters of a winepress. So why on earth would Gideon be threshing wheat in there? The text tells us, "In order to hide it from the Midianites" (Judg. 6:11).

God spoke to Gideon and told him that He wanted Gideon to deliver the Israelites from the hand of the Midianites. But Gideon was hesitant. Even though the Lord greeted him by calling him a "mighty man of valor" (v. 12), Gideon's clan was the weakest in his tribe, and Gideon was the least in his father's house. The Lord repeated the instruction, adding, "Surely I will be with you, and you shall defeat the Midianites as one man" (v. 16).

Even with all that clarity—even with the promise of God's presence— Gideon still asked for confirmation. Gideon still had his doubts and fears.

> Then [Gideon] said to [God], "If now I have found favor in Your sight, then show me a sign that it is You who talk with me. Do not depart from here, I pray, until I come to You and bring out my offering and set it before You."
>
> And [God] said, "I will wait until you come back."
>
> So Gideon went in and prepared a young goat, and unleavened bread from an ephah of flour. The meat he put in a basket, and he

put the broth in a pot; and he brought them out to Him under the terebinth tree and presented them." (vv. 17–19)

What's amazing to me is that Gideon wanted a sign, but he asked God to wait in the delivery of that sign until he cooked Him dinner first. Cooking dinner was no small task in those days. Gideon didn't have a microwave or a refrigerator or even a drive-through. Gideon had to first run out to his flock and field dress a goat. He needed to light a fire. And he had to scurry around and make the dough so he could make some bread. It was a process that required several hours. How crazy is that? The Creator of the universe was asked to wait while a human tried to figure out if it was really God talking to him or not.

Here's what's great about this part of the story for us: God waits.

God waited for Gideon. And God will wait for us too. God didn't condemn Gideon for wanting confirmation—rather, the opposite of that is true. God was okay with it then—and He's okay with it now. God will wait for us to figure out that He's truly talking to us. That's such a great truth. We're told several times in Scripture to wait upon the Lord (Ps. 27:14; Isa. 40:31), but did you know that God waits upon us too?

So Gideon waited for a sign. When the meal was finished cooking, this is what happened when Gideon presented his offering before the Lord:

The Angel of God said to him, "Take the meat and the unleavened bread and lay them on this rock, and pour out the broth." And he did so.

Then the Angel of the LORD put out the end of the staff that was in His hand, and touched the meat and the unleavened bread; and fire rose out of the rock and consumed the meat and the unleavened bread. And the Angel of the LORD departed out of his sight.

Now Gideon perceived that He was the Angel of the LORD. So

Gideon said, "Alas, O Lord GOD! For I have seen the Angel of the LORD face to face."

Then the LORD said to him, "Peace be with you; do not fear, you shall not die." So Gideon built an altar there to the LORD, and called it The-LORD-Is-Peace. To this day it is still in Ophrah of the Abiezrites. (Judg. 6:20–24)

That was Gideon's first confirmation. He prepared a meal and presented it to the Angel of the Lord. The Angel of the Lord touched the end of a stick to it, and fire consumed the meal. What's also interesting about this passage of scripture is that even after the Angel of the Lord left the presence of Gideon, God still spoke to Gideon. I wonder how God spoke to Gideon this second time. It wasn't face-to-face, as He had just done. Was it to Gideon's spirit that He spoke? The text doesn't tell us for sure, but I like to think of this as a further confirmation. Gideon felt peace within his spirit as the Voice of the Lord spoke to his heart.

Shortly after that was when the fleece came into play.

So Gideon said to God, "If You will save Israel by my hand as You have said—look, I shall put a fleece of wool on the threshing floor; if there is dew on the fleece only, and it is dry on all the ground, then I shall know that You will save Israel by my hand, as You have said." And it was so. When he rose early the next morning and squeezed the fleece together, he wrung the dew out of the fleece, a bowlful of water. Then Gideon said to God, "Do not be angry with me, but let me speak just once more: Let me test, I pray, just once more with the fleece; let it now be dry only on the fleece, but on all the ground let there be dew." And God did so that night. It was dry on the fleece only, but there was dew on all the ground. (vv. 36–40)

Wasn't that amazing? You would think that Gideon would have learned his lesson with the first confirmation—the fiery rock. But he asked for another confirmation. You would think that he'd have learned his lesson with the second confirmation—the wet fleece on dry ground. But no, Gideon asked for a third confirmation—the dry fleece on wet ground. This tells me that God is okay when we ask for confirmation.

Still, maybe we need to be careful about asking for too many confirmations. God honored Gideon's request, and that does tell us that God is okay with confirmation, but you wonder if maybe God would have been more pleased if Gideon had just gotten on with the job at God's first marching order. Maybe God sighed and granted the confirmations because this man just wouldn't trust him otherwise. We really don't know because Scripture is silent here about this issue. But we have other scriptures that warn us not to test God (Deut. 6:16 NIV; Matt. 4:7 NIV), so I'd say we are permitted to ask for confirmation, yet we always need to respect the power and graciousness of God within the process.

I love the rest of the story in Judges 7. God told Gideon to call together the men of Israel, thirty-two thousand of them to come and fight the Midianites. But once that huge crowd of soldiers had assembled, God told Gideon that too many men were there, and he should send some of them home. The battle would be too easy with so many. God wanted all of Israel to know without a doubt that it wasn't by might or power; it was by God's Spirit that they were saved. So twenty-two thousand of the soldiers left.

Now there were only ten thousand soldiers remaining. But the army was still too big. So God told Gideon to devise a little test. God told Gideon to have the soldiers go down to the river and get a drink. The men who flopped on their faces in the water were sent home. But the men who remained alert and vigilant, who stayed on one knee and scooped up water into their hands and lapped water like a dog, always on the lookout for enemy soldiers—these were the cream of the crop. So ninety-seven hundred were sent home, and only three hundred soldiers remained.

God said, *Okay Gideon, this is the size of army I like.* "By the three hundred men who lapped I will save you, and deliver the Midianites into your hand" (v. 7).

But even then, Gideon must have had his doubts because God gave Gideon one more confirmation even though Gideon didn't specifically ask for this one. God told Gideon and his servant Purah to go down to the Midian camp at night and just listen. The armies of the Midianites and Amalekites were sprawled out in the valley floor "as numerous as locusts . . . as the sand by the seashore in multitude" (v. 12), but the Lord led Gideon to listen to a particular enemy soldier who'd just had a dream. The soldier told his buddy about it. In his dream, a loaf of bread tumbled into the camp of Midian, struck the man's tent, and the tent collapsed. The man's buddy gasped and said, "This is nothing else but the sword of Gideon the son of Joash, a man of Israel! Into his hand God has delivered Midian and the whole camp" (v. 14).

How's that for confirmation? Gideon knew the outcome of the battle even before the battle started. And I love his response too: "And so it was, when Gideon heard the telling of the dream and its interpretation, . . . he worshiped" (v. 15). When God confirms His word for us, may we also worship Him.

Three Questions to Confirm

Back to our original question: How do we know if God is truly speaking? Here are three questions we can ask to confirm if we've heard a word from God.[1]

1. Does It Line Up with the Bible?

Does the Bible agree with what you have heard God telling you to do? God's voice will never disagree with God's Word. If something that feels like guidance contradicts the revealed Word of God in Scripture, then it is not of the Lord.

A friend of mine is part of a men's group at another church. One man in that group told the others that God led him to have an affair. The false logic he used was this: God is love. God wants us to be happy. The man wasn't happy in his relationship with his wife. But he was happy when he was with this other woman. Therefore, God told him to have an affair.

What would you say to this man?

How about Malachi 2:16, "[God] hates divorce"? God doesn't hate divorced people, but He hates the agony and tearing of relationships that follows divorce.

How about Ephesians 5:25, "Husbands, love your wives, just as Christ also loved the church and gave Himself for her"?

Many people try to find scriptures to support what they believe (or hope) God is saying. Yet the interaction between Jesus and the Pharisees recorded in Matthew 19:3–8 is an example of how this can be dangerous. A group of Pharisees came to Jesus and asked Him if it was lawful for a man to divorce his wife for any old reason. Jesus answered them by quoting Genesis 2:24: "Have you not read that . . . 'a man shall leave his father and mother and be joined to his wife, and the two shall become one flesh?' . . . Therefore what God has joined together, let not man separate" (Matt. 19:4–6).

Jesus explained to them that Moses allowed certificates of divorce to be given because of mankind's hardness of heart (vv. 7–8). But divorce doesn't line up with God's original plan. Moses knew that a man might take a wife, for instance, but abuse her physically and sexually and treat her like a slave, and not like the queen of a home that she was designed to be. So Moses essentially said, "Look. If a husband is going to sin in that manner, then it's better to have the wife go free and be safe. Give her a certificate of divorce."

Jesus saw through to the Pharisees' true intentions. They wanted to know if they could divorce their wives for any old reason, and they wanted to quote Scripture to justify their way of thinking. But Jesus said that divorce doesn't line up with the heart of God. Jesus said, in effect, "If you truly knew the heart of God and read Scripture with the heart of God in mind, then you'd know divorce isn't the best option."

2. Does Godly Counsel Agree?

If you believe God has spoken to you, then submit it to prayerful counsel. What are other believers saying about the matter? Are they hearing the same thing from the Lord?

Proverbs 12:15 says, "The way of a fool is right in his own eyes, but he who heeds counsel is wise."

Proverbs 24:6 says, "For by wise counsel you will wage your own war, and in a multitude of counselors there is safety."

Seeking godly and prayerful counsel is the wise thing to do. But I also offer a couple of caveats with this point.

Sometimes a person will run a matter by counsel, and various factions of people will give contradictory advice. When that happens, that's a clue that the person is not getting godly counsel because God never contradicts Himself. It might be good counsel, but it's not godly counsel.

At other times a person will already have in mind what he wants to do, so he'll go to a trusted mentor and seek counsel, but the advice that the mentor gives is not what the person wants to hear. So the person will say, "Thank you very much," and go to another person, and another person, and so on until at last he hears what he wants to hear. Then he will claim that he's heard from the Lord. Again, that's counsel. But it's not godly counsel.

When you seek godly counsel, this doesn't mean that you've already made up your mind. It means you feel that you've heard from God, and now you're giving it to the Lord with open hands. You're asking trusted

Christians in your life to sincerely pray about the matter along with you and offer wise, biblical input. Maybe you have blinders on that you don't know about. Maybe your godly counselors will be able to discern a matter more ably as objective third parties.

And when you seek godly counsel, you need to hear God first. You're not asking other people to hear God for you. That's what a lot of people do when they ask for counsel, but the Lord wants to have a personal relationship with you. It's up to you to put in the wonderful legwork of building a relationship with Jesus first. You read your Bible. You pray. You listen for the Lord. You fast. You spend time alone with God. Then, after you hear the voice of God, that's the time to seek godly counsel.

3. Does Peace Reign in Your Heart?

The question to ask is, "Do I have peace?" It always takes faith to follow God, but fear has no part in the experience of following God. Fear is from the Enemy. Faith is from the Lord. It took faith for Gideon to follow God as he did. If God is leading, then He will give peace. The way forward may not be completely revealed—in fact, it probably won't be completely revealed. But you will have peace. This is one of the greatest confirmations of God's voice.

Colossians 3:15 is a foundational verse: "And let the peace of God rule in your hearts, to which also you were called in one body; and be thankful."

The word *rule* used here (*brabeuo* in Greek) means so much more than simply to let peace be present in your hearts. This verse is not simply a call to chill out. The word *rule* in the Greek means "to be an umpire." It means "to reign" or "to arbitrate, judge, decide, or control."[2] God's peace should factor in as one of the main decision-making components.

Philippians 4:7 says, "And the peace of God, which surpasses all understanding, will guard your hearts and minds through Christ Jesus." In every godly decision you make, do you know what protects you? The peace of God in your heart and mind. This peace goes beyond our own understanding. The way forward may look difficult, dangerous, or even impossible. Yet God's peace still guards our hearts and minds.

If you have a feeling of unease in your heart and mind about a matter, then God probably does not want you to head down that road. But if God's peace is evident in a matter, then this is one of the main ways we can know if we've heard the voice of God.

Peace from the Lord's Voice

A couple came up to me after a service at church and asked me to pray about their housing situation for their growing family. They were selling their house and simultaneously purchasing another, which can be quite a stressful situation. Their home was already sold, and they'd just put in an offer on the next house. They were excited about the house and were asking for prayer that the deal would close. This was a godly couple, and they weren't simply moving up in the world or trying to get a bigger house. Their needs as a family were changing, and I knew that their new home would become a place of hospitality, prayer, and ministry, just as their old home had been.

I prayed for them, and I'm not quite sure why these thoughts came to me, but I prayed that if they were to have this particular house, then everything would go smoothly. But I also prayed that if the Lord didn't want them to have this particular house, then they would lose peace about the situation and pull out of the deal. At the same time, if the Lord didn't want them to have this particular house, I prayed that He would lead them to the exact home He wanted them in, and that He would give them peace about that situation.

A few months later they contacted me again and filled me in on the rest of the story. They described how they had initially been so excited about the house they'd put an offer on. They were positive this house was their dream home. But after I'd prayed for them, a funny thing happened. They lost all peace over the transaction. Right after that they received news that three large-scale structural issues were wrong with the house. To fix these issues would have cost them a fortune, much more than they were capable of paying. They were able to carefully and legally back out of the deal. Then, just as soon as they pulled out, another house became available. They had deep peace about this house, and they ended up buying it. It turned out to be exactly what they needed.

The Bible indicates that not only is it okay to ask God for confirmation, but it's also wise to ask Him to confirm His word. We can know that it is really God speaking to us by asking Him to confirm His word through the Bible, godly counsel, and the peace in our hearts. It always takes faith to follow God, but when we step out in faith based on a word from Him that has been confirmed, we'll walk in peace.

Is there something you believe God is speaking to you about right now? Pray for clarity and confirmation. Thank God that He is willing to wait for us to make sure we're hearing Him. Thank Him that He wants to speak to us even more than we usually want to hear from Him.

CHAPTER SEVEN

BE A STEWARD OF GOD'S VOICE

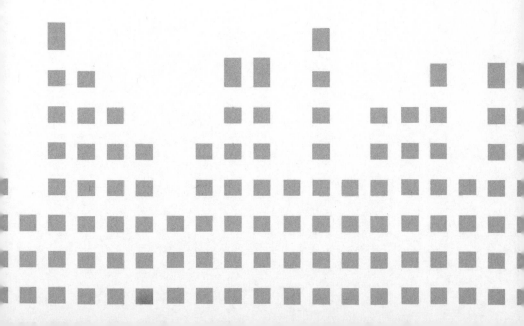

Let all things be done for edification.

—1 Corinthians 14:26

A friend of mine was scheduled to be a guest speaker at a church. He prayerfully prepared a full-length message, the same as he always did. But when he got to the church, he ended up giving one of the most powerful sermons of his life—and it only took two minutes!

The church was small, and the leadership and congregation had well-meaningly developed a tradition of waiting on the Lord during each service to hear from Him. Now, this definitely can be a beneficial and biblical practice, particularly for churches where the service is minimally structured. First Corinthians 14:26 says, "Whenever you come together, each of you has a psalm, has a teaching, has a tongue, has a revelation, has an interpretation. Let all things be done for edification."

Yet the problem at this particular church seemed to be that the idea of waiting on the Lord had morphed into rote tradition only. They'd sing a few worship songs, and then it would get quiet while the congregation waited. Someone would get the bright idea that if they were to get out of there in at least an hour, then someone needed to hear from the Lord pretty quickly. So a person thinking that way would stand up and speak, and there'd be a prophecy in this fashion. Then they'd sing another couple of songs, and it would grow quiet again. Someone else would decide he or she had heard the voice of the Lord and would speak. And so on and so on.

Sure enough, that's what happened this particular Sunday. They sang a couple of songs. It grew quiet. Finally a man stood up and said, "Thus saith the Lord," and spoke a few words. Then the congregation sang a few more songs. It grew quiet again. A woman stood up and said, "This is what the Lord says to us," and spoke a few words. This happened several times.

My friend was sitting on the front pew, praying and carefully taking mental notes. As he began to realize what was happening, his spirit grew troubled. He wondered if the congregation was truly valuing God's voice or if they were only going through the motions. He remembered 1 Corinthians 14:29: "Let two or three prophets speak, and let the others weigh what is said" (ESV). So he chose to obey the word of the Lord directly, weigh what was said, and see if they were truly hearing from the Lord in the service.

When he got up to speak, he opened his Bible and said, "Before I share, I have a question for you." The congregation nodded, and my friend continued, "This morning in the service we have heard three words from the Lord. I wonder if anybody could tell me what the first word was."

Silence.

"All right then," said my friend. "What did God say in the second prophecy?"

Again, silence.

"How about the third message from the Lord? Can anybody remember what the Lord said to us?"

My friend closed his Bible and inhaled deeply, weighing his next words carefully. "I'm sorry," he said. "If you won't listen to God, then you won't listen to me."

He turned around and walked out.

Valuing His Voice

Here's the point: we must value God's voice. We must pay attention. If we truly believe that God is speaking to us, then we must listen closely to the words He says, remember them, and then we must act upon them in humility, faith, and obedience.

Are you familiar with the concept of stewardship? It means that we manage well somebody else's property or resources. As believers, our lives are not our own. We belong to Christ (1 Cor. 3:23). That means our time, treasure, talents, and even our futures are not our own. So it's important that we live as good stewards of what belongs to God. First Peter 4:10 says, "As each has received a gift, use it to serve one another, as good stewards of God's varied grace" (ESV).

Stewardship relates to hearing the voice of God too. Think of it this way. God blesses faithful stewards (Prov. 28:20; Luke 12:42–46). If God gives us time, treasure, and talents, and we're faithful with those, then He gives us more. If we're not faithful, then God doesn't give us more. The same is true of hearing God's voice. When God speaks to us, if we're faithful with the word He gives us, then He will give us more words. But if we're not faithful with the word He gives us, then why would He give us more? Mark 4:24 says, "Take heed what you hear. With the same measure you use, it will be measured to you; and to you who hear, more will be given."

Did you catch the last bit of that verse? "To you who hear, more will be given." That's the result of good stewardship. We must be good stewards of what we hear from the Lord.

How can we be faithful stewards? Let me give you three ways we need to be careful stewards of God's spoken words.

1. We Are Careful Stewards of God's Voice When We Truly Listen to Him

Have you ever heard a catchy song and sung along only to discover later that you were singing the wrong words? What about the first line of Van Morrison's signature song "Brown Eyed Girl"? For years a friend thought the line was, "Hey there, amigo."

We definitely have a listening problem in this generation. We hear so many things—words and songs from TV commercials, the radio, the Internet, movies, music—and we hear these things so quickly that it's difficult to discern what's truly important and to truly listen. Yet when someone important speaks, it's important to listen to Him. God speaks to people who seek to hear Him with humble hearts and to those who will faithfully act upon His spoken word.

God speaks at least ten ways in the Bible. It's important to be aware of these ways, and then to ask ourselves if we are truly listening to Him. Let me give you a short rundown of the ways God speaks as shown in the Bible. In order for us to listen, it's vital that we see not only that God speaks but also how He speaks.

1. **God can speak through circumstances.** God spoke to Jonah first with His voice, but Jonah didn't heed God's voice. So God spoke to Jonah through circumstances—first, being swallowed by a great fish, and second when a vine grew up to shade Jonah, and then the vine withered (Jonah 1–4). We need to examine our circumstances and ask if we are hearing the Lord through these circumstances. Ask yourself two questions: What's happening in my life right now? What is the Lord telling me through these circumstances?

2. **God can speak through wise counsel.** This is shown all through Proverbs.[1] When we seek godly counsel, we can hear the voice of God. This counsel always complements Scripture. When we seek wise, godly mentors in the Lord, we don't ask them to hear from God for us, but to prayerfully confirm that what we've heard from the Lord is correct.

3. **God can speak through peace.** I mentioned Colossians 3:15 in an earlier chapter—that God's peace can rule in our hearts. The word *rule* doesn't simply mean to merely exist. It means to reign or to be a deciding factor. If we don't have peace about a decision, then it isn't from the Lord. Don't move forward unless you have peace.

4. **God can speak through people.** This pattern is shown throughout the Bible.[2] God brings wise and godly people into the lives of others and speaks through them.

5. **God can speak through dreams and visions.** This pattern is shown in the lives of Joseph, Solomon, Jacob, Peter, John, and Paul.[3] This method is available to us today too (see Acts 2:17, where Peter quotes Joel 2:28).

6. **God can speak through our thoughts.** Amos 4:13 says that God makes known His ways to us through our thoughts. In Matthew 1:19–21, while Joseph thought about things, God spoke to him. We need to be careful here because not every thought in our minds comes from the Lord. Thoughts can also be placed in our minds from the Devil. And we can simply think up things on our own. So every time we get a thought, we need to judge if it is from God. Does it align with Scripture? Does it in any way contradict the character of God?

7. **God can speak through natural manifestations.** Romans 1:18–20 states clearly that God can make Himself known by nature. The voice of God can be revealed through mountains, water, trees, meadows, landscapes, and more. In John 12:27–30, God spoke from heaven, but when God spoke in this incident, some people who stood nearby thought they were hearing thunder.

8. **God can speak through supernatural manifestations.** God spoke to Moses through a burning bush (Ex. 3:1–4). He spoke to Gideon through a fleece (Judg. 6:37–40). He spoke to Saul on the Damascus road through a bright light (Acts 9:1–5). He even spoke to Balaam through a donkey (Num. 22:1–35).

9. **God can speak through the Bible.** Scripture is always the voice of God in the general sense that God inspired the words of Scripture (2 Tim. 3:16). God can also speak specifically

to us through the Bible by drawing a particular passage to our attention, because the Word of God is living and active (Heb. 4:12).

10. **God can speak through a whisper.** We discussed in an earlier chapter how God can speak through a still small voice. He spoke this way to Elijah (1 Kings 19:12).

Again, the point here is that if we are going to hear God's voice, then we need to listen to Him. We need to tune in to the frequency of heaven and hear the voice of God. Note the warning held out in Jeremiah 7:13: "While you have been sinning, I have been trying to talk to you, but you refuse to listen" (CEV). Essentially, God is saying to the Israelites that they did any number of wicked things, and He was speaking and speaking to them repeatedly about it, but they did not listen to Him.

I love the promise held out for us in Romans 10:17: "So then faith comes by hearing, and hearing by the word of God." If you've ever met a person of great faith, then you've met a person of great hearing who knows how to listen to the Word of God.

We need to truly listen to God. Once we hear from Him, then we need to act in faith. Have you heard from God and truly listened to His voice? Then good; now is the time to move with confidence.

2. We Are Careful Stewards of God's Voice When We Respond in Humility

If a person hears from God and then responds with pride, or dishes out the word with a haughty spirit, then this is not a careful stewardship of God's message to us. Similarly, a person can hear God's voice yet respond with closed ears. Or a person can hear God's word and initially respond favorably, but then the cares of life can choke the response. These patterns are also not good stewardship.

Luke 8:4–15, the parable of the sower, provides a good foundation for understanding receptivity to God's word. The sower casts seeds on four types of ground. Some of the seed fell by the wayside and was trampled underfoot and devoured by birds. Some of the seed fell on rocky soil and soon sprang up but withered because it lacked moisture. Some of the seed fell among thorns; it sprang up, but then the thorns choked it. And finally some of the seed fell on good ground. It sprang up and yielded a crop of a hundredfold. What kind of ground are you? Do you have thorns? Are you rocky? Are you parched and lacking spiritual nutrients? Or are you receptive?

Luke 8:18 holds out a warning for us: "Therefore take heed how you hear. For whoever has, to him more will be given; and whoever does not have, even what he seems to have will be taken from him."

Two parts of this verse warrant closer examination. The parable of the sower, found in Luke, was talking about what we hear. But Luke 8:18 exhorts us to "take heed how you hear." In other words, Jesus is telling us to watch how we receive His word. We are to make sure our ground is tilled and free of thorns to help ensure bountiful growth. We are to make sure we are humble when we receive the word of God. We are to ensure that we are pliable ground.

The last part of Luke 8:18 also contains a powerful clause, "Even what he seems to have will be taken from him." Plenty of Christians fail to produce abundant growth. The seed of the word of God might continually be falling on their ground, but unless their soil is watered and weeded, then even the spiritual maturity that seems to be evident can be lost.

Are you familiar with the story of Joseph in Genesis 37? Joseph was only seventeen when he began to hear from God in dreams. Yet when he told his first dream to his brothers, he told it with a haughty spirit (or perhaps he simply told it carelessly) because his brothers hated him for it and were jealous. Joseph had another dream from God and told it to his parents, and they also responded unfavorably. Envy was produced in the family, and Joseph's "father rebuked him" for it (v. 10).

Joseph's dreams were clearly from God. But Joseph's reactions might not have been from God. Why did he even need to tell his brothers about the first dream? The dream was all about the brothers bowing down to Joseph one day. A prudent young man might do well to keep that sort of information to himself. And why did Joseph tell his parents about the second dream? It was all about his parents bowing down to him one day. You'd think Joseph would have learned his lesson from the reaction he got when he told the brothers about the first dream.

I believe Joseph may have told others about his dream because of his pride. It certainly wasn't a wise decision. At the least, it was probably youthful indiscretion. Here's the amazing thing: God never spoke to Joseph in a dream again—never, not one time. God gave Joseph two dreams when he was young to see how he'd handle them, but Joseph squandered the opportunity. He immediately went out and bragged about the dreams; he did not guard them carefully and cherish them in his heart. There he could have pondered them more fully as did Mary with God's message to her and the miracles surrounding Jesus' birth (Luke 2:19).

Fortunately, God did a lot of work in Joseph's life as he grew up, and Joseph responded well to the tutelage. Later on Joseph was able to interpret the dreams of others, and that helped lead him to his destiny. If we squander opportunities when we're young (or even later on in life), God isn't through with us yet. God is always the God of the comeback. Yet it's very important that when God speaks to us, we don't use God's word to make ourselves look better.

James 4:6–7 says, "But He gives more grace. Therefore He says: 'God resists the proud, but gives grace to the humble.' Therefore submit to God. Resist the devil and he will flee from you." I love that verse! God promises that He gives us grace. And then He gives us more grace still. And the implication is that if we need even more grace after that, then He'll give us that too! But the teaching doesn't stop there. A warning is found. The Bible says, "God resists the proud." It means that if we are prideful, then God is resisting us. In the original Greek, the word for *resist* means "to oppose."[4] It's a sports word where two teams are said to oppose each other when they play on a field together.

Picture a game of football. If we are believers, then God lets us run with the ball. We even get to make touchdowns. We get to teach. We get to lead. We get to minister. We get to give. We get to serve. We get to be part of God's amazing plan for His kingdom. And the great thing about being on God's team is that He runs ahead of us, clearing our way forward. It's as though He says, *Hey, just stay behind Me all the way. I've got this. Just follow Me.*

But if we are proud, instead of us running unhindered, we are tackled and pushed back by opposition. Our ministry is hampered. In the case of James 4:6–7, the opposition is actually God. What might God's opposition look like? If we are proud, then we start to think we know a lot about football. We say to God, "Don't worry about this one. I've run the ball plenty of times before. You can sit this one out, God." Our minds may be thinking, *I'm a pretty great football player. Everybody in the stands is cheering for me.*

With this mind-set it becomes much more difficult to see the people we pray for find freedom. It's much more difficult to effectively lead a small group or teach a Sunday school class. It's hard to see real spiritual change effected in the lives of others. If we're prideful, then it's as if God says, "Okay, you want to do this on your own. Then let's see how far you get."

Humility is very important in being stewards of the word of God.

3. We Are Careful Stewards of God's Voice When We Heed His Words

Remember Jonah? It's a classic case of disobedience there. Jonah heard from the Lord, but what did Jonah do? He ran the other way. God told Jonah to go to Nineveh, but Jonah jumped on a boat heading for Tarshish. God said go north, but Jonah went south.

So God caused a storm. Jonah got thrown into the sea and was swallowed by a huge fish. There, in the belly of the fish, Jonah cried out to the Lord his God. Jonah repented. He basically said, "God, I was wrong. If I could turn this fish around and go to Nineveh, I'd do that."

Earlier in this chapter I touched briefly on the subject of God's using circumstances to speak to people. Jonah's story provides an example of that. Jonah clearly heard from the Lord, but Jonah did not heed God's voice. So God set into motion circumstances that would convey the message more strongly to Jonah. Mark this carefully: I have people tell me that they aren't hearing God's voice. When that happens, I tell them to look at their circumstances, and then go back to the last thing God clearly said to them and see if they obeyed or not. If they can't remember, then I encourage them to simply do what Jonah did: repent. Stop going your way and go God's way instead.

Here's the big question: If God spoke to you, did you do it? Obedience is so important in the life of a believer. And I'm not talking about just gritting our teeth and trying harder. God gives us the power to obey by His Holy Spirit, and His way forward is always the way of grace. Obedience is mandatory in God's economy. Jesus offers these straightforward words to His disciples in John 14:15, "If you love Me, keep My commandments." The apostle John apparently understood this message explicitly, for he repeated it later on in the Bible in 1 John 5:3, "For this is the love of God, that we keep His commandments. And His commandments are not burdensome."

The process of us being obedient to God has been compared to a surfer learning to catch a wave. The power of the ocean is like the Holy Spirit in our lives. When a surfer paddles out to sea, the power of the wave actually does the main work in bringing him to shore again. Yet the surfer must align himself with the power of the ocean. He must position his board so he can catch the power of the wave. He must paddle with the power of the ocean, not against it, if he wants to ride successfully to land. This is true of us and God. The Holy Spirit ultimately makes us holy. His work and power ultimately transform our lives. Our job is to continually align ourselves with Him and yield ourselves to His work and power.

Blessing the Lord

I wonder if you've ever thought about why we need to be careful stewards of God's voice. I mean, sure, the reason is to obey God, and it's so God doesn't shut down that area of blessing for us. But is there an even greater reason, one that's God-focused, not us-focused?

One day early in our ministry, Debbie and I were driving down the road and we saw a bumper sticker that said, "Come bless the Lord." It was from a church called Shady Grove Church, and I'd never heard of that church back then. Shady Grove Church, in the 1980s, would sometimes have two to three hours of worship before the message, and powerful things were going on there—changed hearts and lives, new beginnings, even healings. Are you old enough to remember the song "We Bring the Sacrifice of Praise"?[5] It came out of Shady Grove Church in that era.

But I remember when I first saw that bumper sticker, I sort of turned to Debbie with a harrumph and said, "Look at that audacity. Why would a church ever think that God would be blessed by what it does or if you attend there? We don't bless God. God blesses us."

Now, I know the Lord heard me say that. And I don't know if this is part of His holy sense of humor or not because pretty soon Debbie and I were attending that church ourselves. And pretty soon after that, I was on staff there. The Lord led me to study the Scriptures, and I soon learned that it's very biblical, indeed, not only for God to bless us but for us to bless God too.

The word *bless* in the original Greek is *makarios*. It means happy.[6]
Here are some of the scriptures God led me to:

> I will bless the LORD at all times;
> His praise shall continually be in my mouth.
> > —Psalm 34:1

> Bless God in the congregations.
> > —Psalm 68:26

> Bless the LORD, O my soul,
> And forget not all His benefits.
> > —Psalm 103:2

> The dead do not praise the LORD,
> Nor any who go down into silence.
> But we will bless the LORD
> From this time forth and forevermore.
>
> Praise the LORD!
> > —Psalm 115:17–18

> Behold, bless the LORD,
> All you servants of the LORD,
> Who by night stand in the house of the LORD!
> Lift up your hands in the sanctuary,
> And bless the LORD.
> > —Psalm 134:1–2

What's the ultimate reason for being careful stewards of God's voice? It's to bless Him. We can actually minister to the Lord when we worship Him and handle His word with care.

Note the close connection in Acts 13:1–5, between blessing the Lord and hearing the Lord's voice:

> Now in the church that was at Antioch there were certain prophets and teachers: Barnabas, Simeon who was called Niger, Lucius of Cyrene, Manaen who had been brought up with Herod the tetrarch, and Saul. *As they ministered to the Lord and fasted, the Holy Spirit said,* "Now separate to Me Barnabas and Saul for the work to which I have called them." Then, having fasted and prayed, and laid hands on them, they sent them away.
>
> So, being sent out by the Holy Spirit, they went down to Seleucia, and from there they sailed to Cyprus. And when they arrived in Salamis, they preached the word of God in the synagogues of the Jews. They also had John as their assistant.

Five men ministered to the Lord by fasting and praying. Within that fasting and praying, the Holy Spirit spoke to them and called two of them to a specific, new work. These men took the gospel to the Gentiles, and eventually the gospel spread all over the world. The Holy Spirit spoke as the five ministered to the Lord.

How do we minister to the Lord? It involves far more than singing a few songs each Sunday. We minister to God when we acknowledge who He truly is. We worship Him. We praise His name. We delight in developing a relationship with Him. We listen to His words. As good stewards, we carefully handle whatever He tells us.

A Lunch Conversation

Debbie and I were in New Zealand, ministering in some churches there. One day one of our host pastors and his wife invited us out for lunch.

When the waitress came to take our order, we noticed she didn't speak with a New Zealand accent. So we asked her where she was from, and she said the United States. She and her husband had just moved to New Zealand.

Our conversation was a quick exchange, and the restaurant was busy with the lunch rush, so that was about all that was said. But it was funny because when the waitress was speaking to us, I had the distinct impression upon my heart that we were to invite her and her husband to church. But you know how it goes. I wondered if I was truly hearing from the Lord, and we got busy with our lunch and talking with the other couple. When we were finished with lunch, a different waitress brought us our check. I was pretty sure I couldn't do anything about the invitation now, so we all left.

While standing in the parking lot, talking to the pastor and his wife, I got the same distinct impression that I was to invite the waitress and her husband to church, but now the impression was even stronger. This time I chose to obey. "Would you excuse me for a moment?" I said to the others. "I've got a bit of unfinished work to attend to." And I headed back into the restaurant.

I found the hostess and inquired about our waitress. It turned out that she had gone on break, which is why someone else brought our check to us. I asked if I could speak with her anyway. The hostess went into the back to find her, and our waitress soon came out.

"I'm sorry," I said, when she appeared. "I know you need your break. But I just have this strong impression that I'm supposed to invite you and your husband to come to church this weekend."

Her face lit up and she responded, "I can't believe you said that. My husband and I have never gone to church except for a few times when we were kids. But we've been over here for three months now, and we just started talking about the need to meet some people, and as we discussed it together, one of us said, 'Why don't we start going to a church to meet some people?'"

I was able to give her the name and address of a good, Christ-centered, Bible-teaching church nearby. I was so glad I obeyed God (isn't that always the case!). She might have gone to a church that didn't even preach the gospel.

My friends, God is always speaking in many ways. In Mark 4:24, Jesus warned His disciples, "Take heed what you hear. With the same measure you use, it will be measured to you; and to you who hear, more will be given." Good stewardship means to manage someone else's resources well. We tend to think of stewardship as managing our time and money, but Jesus' warning in Mark tells us that we're responsible to steward God's spoken word as well. Those who listen to God—receive His word with humble hearts and act upon it—will hear God again. But James 4:6 tells us, "God resists the proud." God will not continue to speak to prideful people or those who do not obey what He has said.

God is speaking all the time, but the only ones who hear are those who tune in to the right frequency through humility and obedience.

May we be those who steward God's word well. Amen.

CHAPTER EIGHT

RECOGNIZE GOD'S VOICE THROUGH RELATIONSHIP

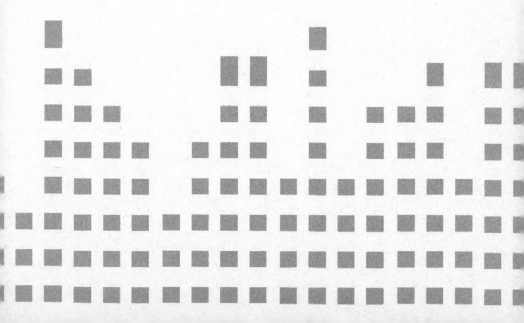

The Spirit Himself bears witness with our spirit
that we are children of God, and if children, then
heirs—heirs of God and joint heirs with Christ.
—Romans 8:16-17

When our children were younger, Debbie and I didn't have much money. We lived in a tiny house with one tiny bathroom. But we did have one luxury—a hot tub on our back porch. The hot tub wasn't very big. Only two people could fit in it. It was so unsophisticated that to heat it up you simply plugged it into a regular wall socket. Every night after we put the kids to bed, Debbie and I would sit in our hot tub and talk. The stores had just come out with baby monitors back then (that's how long ago it was), and we'd place one end of our baby monitor in the baby's room and the other end near the hot tub so we could hear if the baby cried. One time the monitor actually fell into the hot tub. But it was amazing because after that, the baby never cried again.

One evening during our hot-tub talk, Debbie turned very serious and said to me, "Robert, I want to ask you something."

I nodded. I'd just been teaching some Bible classes on hearing God's voice, and she said, "Would you personally teach me how to hear God?"

"Sure," I said. We went through some general principles from the Bible, and then I added, "You know, you can hear God right now; did you know that? Let's just stop for a moment and focus on the Lord and pray and ask God to speak to you. He'll speak; I promise. It'll be like a thought coming into your mind that aligns with the character and goodness of God. Ready?"

So Debbie nodded, and we closed our eyes, and I prayed. Then I opened my eyes, and I watched her face. She looked as though she was listening really intently. Then she kind of tilted her head, smiled, and shrugged all at the same time, as if to say, "Oh well."

"Wait a minute," I said. "What did you just hear?"

"Well, it wasn't God," she said. "I know that."

"How do you know?" I asked. "Tell me what you just heard."

She paused, as if searching for the right words, then began. "Well, right before I put the kids to bed, I read them that old children's story, *The Little Engine That Could*. You remember it? It's about a little blue train engine that was designed to pull small things, like one or two cars around a rail yard. There was a long train that needed to be pulled over a mountain. So the long train asked several big engines if they could pull it over the hill, but all of the big engines said no. So finally the long train went to the little engine and asked him. The little engine said yes, and the whole time it worked at the job, it kept repeating this phrase over and over and over again, 'I think I can, I think I can, I think I can.' And finally it got over the hill. And then it said, 'I know I can, I know I can, I know I can.'[1] That's what I heard just now. I heard that phrase. But that couldn't be from God, could it?"

As I listened to my wife, I was praying simultaneously, and when she said that, the Holy Spirit immediately impressed upon my heart that this was indeed the voice of God for her.

"You just heard God," I said. "You see yourself as the little engine and me as the big engine, and the Lord is trying to tell you that you can hear from the Lord yourself. It's not 'I think I can, I think I can,' but 'I know I can, I know I can.'"

Years have passed since then, and my wife has developed her personal relationship with God over time and grown deeper in her faith. These days, whenever she comes to me and says, "Robert, I have a word from the Lord for you," I'm all ears because she regularly hears from the Lord today.

Maybe you're at that same stage in your spiritual journey where you don't know whether or not you can hear from the Lord. You've read this far in this book, and you're saying, "Well, I think I can do this." I want to encourage you that you can indeed hear from the Lord. It's not "I think I can, I think I can," but "I know I can, I know I can."

The key to hearing the Lord regularly is to grow in our relationship with the Lord. We never need to hide from God or be distant from God. Jesus paid for all our sins, and so those sins are no longer blocking our access. We can learn to recognize God's voice when we spend a lot of time with God. Hebrews 4:16 offers us a wonderful invitation: "Let us therefore come boldly to the throne of grace, that we may obtain mercy and find grace to help in time of need."

A Personal Relationship with the Lord

When people think about the gospel, sometimes the only word that comes to mind is *forgiveness*. This idea is easy to grasp and to appreciate for a person who realizes he's a sinner, or particularly for a person who's led an immoral life before coming to Jesus. God has wiped the slate clean. God gives people a fresh start.

Certainly forgiveness is a big part of the gospel. Passage after passage of Scripture talks about the forgiveness of God for our sins. Isaiah 1:18 is one of my favorites.

> "Come now, and let us reason together,"
> Says the LORD,
> "Though your sins are like scarlet,
> They shall be as white as snow;
> Though they are red like crimson,
> They shall be as wool."

But have you ever thought about how the gospel involves more than forgiveness?[2] It includes reconciliation, a big word that simply means things are put back together again. For instance, after a husband and wife have an argument, they make up and come to an understanding.

We say that they're reconciled again. Their relationship is harmonious. We find the idea that we are reconciled to God spiritually because of Jesus Christ in 2 Corinthians 5:18–19, among other places:

> Now all things are of God, who has reconciled us to Himself through Jesus Christ, and has given us the ministry of reconciliation, that is, that God was in Christ reconciling the world to Himself, not imputing their trespasses to them, and has committed to us the word of reconciliation.

Another fantastic passage is Romans 5:10: "For if when we were enemies we were reconciled to God through the death of His Son, much more, having been reconciled, we shall be saved by His life."

Maybe reconciliation sounds too clinical to you. The idea seems too conceptual or cerebral to get excited about or too difficult to get your mind around. That's why God gives us stories in the Bible. Jesus often told parables, which are simple stories with a meaning. Why? Because sometimes it can be easier for us to see and feel the wonder of a truth through the lens of a story. The story that teaches both the idea of forgiveness and reconciliation is the parable of the prodigal son (Luke 15:11–32).

Remember the parable? A certain man had two sons. The younger son asked the father for his inheritance early. Then the younger son went away and squandered all he had on wild living. After the younger son finally came to his senses, he put his tail between his legs and traveled home to his father, hoping simply that the father would make him one of his hired hands. We read this wonderful description of the homecoming:

> But when [the younger son] was still a great way off, his father saw him and had compassion, and ran and fell on his neck and kissed him. And the son said to him, "Father, I have sinned against heaven and in your sight, and am no longer worthy to be called your son."

But the father said to his servants, "Bring out the best robe and put it on him, and put a ring on his hand and sandals on his feet. And bring the fatted calf here and kill it, and let us eat and be merry; for this my son was dead and is alive again; he was lost and is found." And they began to be merry. (vv. 20–24)

See, when it comes to the gospel, God does not simply forgive us; He reconciles us to Himself. The Father doesn't simply say, "The slate is clean; you can earn your keep in My employ and be My lowly servant." No. The Father spreads wide His arms and says, "Come on home. Here's the best robe for you to wear. Here's a ring for your hand and sandals for your feet. You are My child. And you're home at last! Everything I have is yours. It's time to party!"

That's the gospel!

That's why a personal relationship with Jesus is so wonderful. We're not merely forgiven by God. We're reconciled to God. Through the work of Jesus on the cross, our relationship with God is made harmonious again. The apostle Paul could hardly contain himself when he wrote about this truth:

For this reason I bow my knees to the Father of our Lord Jesus Christ, from whom the whole family in heaven and earth is named, that He would grant you, according to the riches of His glory, to be strengthened with might through His Spirit in the inner man, that Christ may dwell in your hearts through faith; that you, being rooted and grounded in love, may be able to comprehend with all the saints what is the width and length and depth and height—to know the love of Christ which passes knowledge; that you may be filled with all the fullness of God.

Now to Him who is able to do exceedingly abundantly above all that we ask or think, according to the power that works in us, to Him be glory in the church by Christ Jesus to all generations, forever and ever. Amen. (Eph. 3:14–21)

What's my point? I want you to know what truly happened to you when you chose to follow Jesus. I want you to know and feel that the Father loves you deeply and intensely. God has welcomed you home with open arms. We are sons and daughters of God (Rom. 8:16–17). We are heirs according to the promise (Gal. 3:29). Everything the Father has is ours (Luke 15:31). We have every spiritual blessing in Christ (Eph. 1:3). That's what a personal relationship with Jesus is all about!

It's a wonderful general principle that when our personal relationship with Jesus is deepened, then we can hear His voice better. How can we recognize the voice of God? How can we know for sure that God is talking, and we're not just thinking our own thoughts? We can recognize the voice of God when we are in a deep relationship with Him. The depth of our relationship with God is the foundation for knowing His voice.

There's one caveat. Sometimes a person in a deep relationship with God will be trusted with a time of God's silence. This person may be walking closely and carefully with the Lord, but will experience no communication that can be recognized as from God, other than the Bible itself. But it may be that the person is simply being led by God through a time of testing. God may be saying, "Can you trust Me when you don't hear from Me at all?"

Remember the story of Abraham as recorded in Genesis? He was called a "friend of God" (James 2:23), and we're told he "believed God, and it was credited to him as righteousness" (Gal. 3:6 NIV). So certainly he had a deep relationship with the Lord. Yet only a few times in his life does Abraham hear the voice of God, and there are long stretches of silence in between, sometimes decades.

Job is another example of a man in a deep relationship with God who experienced God's silence. God Himself told Satan that Job was "a blameless and upright man, one who fears God and shuns evil" (Job 1:8). But Job went through an excruciating time of God's silence coupled with difficult trials. His friends babbled platitudes, but God did not speak for a long, long time. Certainly God could have broken through and spoken to Job much sooner, as He finally does near the end of the recorded story, but first Job had to go through the full time of testing.

Having pointed out exceptions, we need to remind ourselves that it's generally true that the closer our relationship with God, the better we are able to hear His voice. It's of great benefit to us to deepen our fellowship with the Lord, and one benefit is that we are able to hear Him more readily when He chooses to speak to us.

So I want to offer three truths about having a personal relationship with God. These truths help us know how to hear the voice of God.

1. Our Relationship with God Must Be Our Highest Priority

Are you familiar with the lyrics to the old hymn "My Jesus I Love Thee"? A teenager named William Featherstone first wrote the lyrics as a poem in the 1800s. Later, Adoniram Judson Gordon (founder of Gordon College and Gordon-Conwell Theological Seminary) set the poem to music.

The second line of the first verse as it's usually sung today is "For Thee all the follies of sin I resign." But that word *follies* is actually a later change to the song. In the original version, the word was *pleasures*. "For Thee all the pleasures of sin I resign." There's something keenly profound about that original word being associated with sin.[3]

See, the big lie that sin holds out for us is that it's truly pleasurable. Oh, sin might be pleasurable for a moment or two, but it's never truly satisfying—not in a fulfilling, lasting, honorable way. In Genesis 3, when the serpent came to Adam and Eve in the garden of Eden, he held out this old lie: "It's more pleasurable to disobey God than to obey

Him. Things are going to go better for you if you eat the fruit than if you don't. Somehow you're missing something. God is withholding something good from you. Sin is the solution."

Satan has no new tricks. He whispers the same lie to us today: "Sin is the solution. If you sin, then you will have joy. You will have peace. You will have pleasure." But the very thing that Satan tells us to do so that we will be happy is actually the very thing that will cause us to lose what we already have. We don't lose our salvation, but we lose our close fellowship with God. Adam and Eve already enjoyed close harmony with God. He hadn't withheld anything good from them. But when we sin, the sin muddies the relationship, and we lose the close relationship with God that we can enjoy.

Listen. If you have Jesus, you will have joy. You will have peace. You will have lasting satisfaction. That's why we must make our relationship with God our highest priority. Jesus invites us to follow Him closely, to exchange the superficial pleasures of sin for the true, deep, and lasting pleasures of knowing Him. Certainly when we sin, grace is always available. Jesus forgives us, and He reconciles us to Him time and time again. But we don't need to go through the pain of sin in order to experience reconciliation. How much better it is never to stray from a close walk with God. "What shall we say then? Shall we continue in sin that grace may abound? Certainly not! How shall we who died to sin live any longer in it?" (Rom. 6:1–2).

One of the things that happened when Adam and Eve sinned relates directly to hearing God's voice. In the beginning God created Paradise and set two young people in the midst of that Paradise. Every morning and evening, in the cool of the day, God would meet with them. I like to think it was more than a mere conversation—even though a conversation with God would have been great enough by itself. I think God enjoyed Paradise with them. God enjoyed showing them around the garden. Maybe God, Adam, and Eve hiked for a few miles, and then God showed them a new, huge three-hundred-foot waterfall. Everybody jumped in for a swim. Then maybe God said, *Come on, I'll show you a herd of elephants. There—just over the rise. Aren't they funny with their long trunks and big ears?* And maybe sometimes their conversations were like those quiet, almost breathless words that can be whispered between a husband and wife when they're perfectly at peace, lying side by side, holding hands, drifting off to sleep—perfect harmony, perfect intimacy, perfect joy, perfect peace.

But then Adam and Eve sinned. And fear entered the picture.

And they heard the sound of the LORD God walking in the garden in the cool of the day, and Adam and his wife hid themselves from the presence of the LORD God among the trees of the garden.

Then the LORD God called to Adam and said to him, "Where are you?"

So [Adam] said, "I heard Your voice in the garden, and I was afraid because I was naked; and I hid myself." (Gen. 3:8–10)

Think about that passage. Maybe God had the whole day planned for Adam and Eve, same as always. But He went looking for them and couldn't find them because they were hiding from Him. God heard the saddest words He'd ever heard:

"I heard Your voice . . .
I was afraid . . .
and I hid."

Fear is where the problems all started. The relationship was damaged. The harmonious communication was rudely interrupted. When sin came into the world, people began to fear the voice of God. Adam had never feared God's voice before—never. But sin changed everything and separated Adam from God.

Here's the good news. Jesus restored that relationship—us with God. We don't need to hide ourselves from God anymore. We can still hear God's voice clearly today, without separation, without fear. We don't ever need to be afraid when God speaks to us because Jesus repaired the relationship.

That's why our relationship with God must be our highest priority. We are dead to sin and alive to Christ.

2. Our Relationship with God Must Be Our Highest Pursuit

Our relationship with God must be both our highest priority and our highest pursuit.

Priority refers to what we deem as having the highest importance.

Pursuit means what we follow closely. If we pursue something, we run after it. We strive for it with all our might.

Back in the garden of Eden, there were actually two named trees that God kept in the middle of the garden. But only one was forbidden. Do you know what they were?

The first was called "the tree of the knowledge of good and evil," and God said Adam and Eve shouldn't eat from its fruit (Gen. 2:16–17). The fruit from this tree alone was actually forbidden. The second was called "the tree of life" (v. 9). It was positioned in proximity to the tree of the knowledge of good and evil in the middle of the garden. If a person ate from the tree of life, the Bible describes the result as immortality; the person would live forever (3:22).

Here is a bold statement: God never intended us to live by the knowledge of good and evil—never. He intended us to eat from the tree of life. God always chooses life. God didn't intend for people to need to live by their consciences and continually weigh what's good and bad. He originally intended people to live by His voice (Matt. 4:4).

Casting doubt on this plan was part of Satan's original lie. He wanted Adam and Eve to believe that sin was more pleasurable than following God, and he wanted Adam and Eve to doubt the voice of God. Remember how several of Satan's temptations began with a question: What did God say? Has God truly said . . . ? (Gen. 3:1) Satan wanted Adam and Eve to doubt God's voice. Once Satan got them to doubt God's voice, then it was easy for Adam and Eve to take the next step and sin. But God wants us to hear His voice. He wants His children to listen to Him. He wants His sheep to hear the voice of the Shepherd. He wants us to rely on hearing and heeding His voice.

Let me say it another way. It might sound shocking, but let me explain. God doesn't want us to live by our consciences, even today. What does the conscience do? It reminds us of the knowledge of good and evil. Certainly a conscience can play a part in our lives, if our consciences are guided by God and redeemed by God. But sometimes our conscience doesn't agree with God. We can't rely only on conscience.

For instance, a person can feel falsely guilty about something. We see this in combat veterans who return from war. Maybe a buddy of theirs died, but they lived, so they feel guilty for living. That's false guilt. Or a conscience can be overactive, prompting a sensitive person to feel condemned, crushed by the weight of sin, even after a person has confessed the sin to the Lord.

The best thing a conscience can ever do is tell us what's good and bad and help bring us to the place of conviction of sin where we know we need Jesus as our Savior. The Holy Spirit picks up the job and brings us to the place of full conviction where we accept the Savior. Then, when Jesus enters our lives, our consciences are cleansed by the blood of Jesus so that we don't serve God out of dead works. Are you familiar with dead works? This is how some people try to earn God's favor. We know that sin separates us from God, so we try to work our way back to Him, as if our effort can save us. Mark this carefully: we can never earn our salvation. We can only receive it. But if our consciences have not been cleansed, then we'll continually work to earn God's favor.

Hebrews 9:14 is a wonderfully freeing verse: "How much more shall the blood of Christ, who through the eternal Spirit offered Himself without spot to God, cleanse your conscience from dead works to serve the living God?"

According to that verse, what does the blood of Jesus do? It cleanses our consciences from dead works. We are free to love Jesus wholeheartedly, to pursue Him with all our hearts, and to serve the living God out of faith, love, and hope (1 Thess. 1:3).

When we follow Christ, it's not even our consciences that actually convict us of right and wrong. That's the job of the Holy Spirit living inside of us. He may sometimes use the natural faculty of the conscience, but He goes above and beyond. Jesus said of the Holy Spirit in John 16:8–11, "And when He has come, He will convict the world of sin, and of righteousness, and of judgment: of sin, because they do not believe in Me; of righteousness, because I go to My Father and you see Me no more; of judgment, because the ruler of this world is judged."

Let me give you a picture of this in action. Once I took some young married couples on a retreat. One of the husbands had only been saved for about three weeks. We were all sitting around the campfire sharing our testimonies, and the newly saved guy asked to share his testimony. Everybody said yes, so he started sharing his testimony. As he talked, he reached into his pocket, pulled out a cigarette, and lit it up.

It was definitely something you just don't see in church every day. I mean, here was this guy, telling us how much he loved Jesus and was so excited to follow Him, and in between sentences he's puffing away on a Marlboro.

I sat back with a slight smile on my face, listening to the man's testimony and quietly observing the other couples around me. A number of them had been Christians for a long time, and I could tell they were uncomfortable. They were sort of murmuring, "What do we do? Should we say something?"

That's conscience at work.

The funny thing was that the longer I looked at the other couples, my conscience started to go to work too. I started thinking that maybe I should say something. I was the leader, after all. I wondered if I should break into the guy's testimony mid-stride and tell him that he needed to quit smoking. But then the Holy Spirit spoke to me in my heart.

Hey, Robert, I've got this.

Don't worry.

Don't ignore what's truly happening in this man's life.

I'll take care of this.

I've saved him. And I'll sanctify him too. But I'll do that in My time and in My way.

I started arguing with the Holy Spirit, saying, "Yeah, but what if You don't convict him of this? The other people in the group won't know that You talked to me and told me just to let this guy continue with telling his testimony."

And God said, *Well, if I don't tell him it's wrong, Robert, then why would you ever tell him?*

Friends, God wants us to live by His voice, not our consciences. Yes, we are to keep our consciences pure (1 Tim. 1:5; 2 Tim. 1:3). But the emphasis always must be on hearing God's voice.

Here's one more way to think about it. What if God told you to do something that violated your conscience? I was talking to a woman once about this subject, and she said, "You know, I don't think I could ever do anything that violated my conscience. God would never do that."

I asked her, "Do you mean that the Eternal Creator and Sustainer of the universe is limited to your conscience? What about the story of Abraham being asked by God to sacrifice his son Isaac?"

We know the end of the story with Abraham and Isaac, and we see in hindsight that God wanted to make sure that Abraham was pursuing Him above all else. My point was that we aren't primarily to be guided by our consciences. We are to be guided by God's voice. This is one reason why our relationship with God must be our highest pursuit.

3. Our Relationship with God Must Be Our Highest Passion

Our relationship with God must be our highest priority, our highest pursuit, and our highest passion.

Priority means what we deem as having the highest importance.

Pursuit means what we follow most closely. If we pursue something, we run after it. We strive for it with all our might.

Passion means that it stirs our greatest feelings of love and devotion. We pursue something because we are passionate about it. Our motivation springs from our passion.

I love the story of Mary and Martha. Luke 10:38–42 describes how when Jesus came to the village called Bethany, the two sisters Mary and Martha welcomed him into their home. Martha took care of all the preparations. She cleaned the house. She cooked the meal. She washed the dishes. She set the table. But Mary sat at the feet of Jesus and listened to His voice, or "heard His word" (v. 39).

Martha grew upset with Mary and complained to Jesus about it.

"Jesus answered and said to her, 'Martha, Martha, you are worried and troubled about many things. But one thing is needed, and Mary has chosen that good part, which will not be taken away from her'" (vv. 41–42).

A key phrase in those verses is "one thing is needed."

Let me ask you this: Are you, like Martha, worried and troubled about many things? If you are, then those things will stop you from sitting down at Jesus' feet and listening to His word. You'll go to open your Bible, but your mind will be elsewhere. Or maybe you won't open your Bible. Reading it will be the last thing on your to-do list for the day, the item that you never get to. Or maybe meeting with Jesus isn't on your radar at all. You're a Christian, but just like thousands of people over the years, you want your pastor to have a personal relationship with God for you.

Our relationship with God must be our highest passion. And we must prioritize our relationship with Him for it to be this way. We must choose to put God first. We must strategically place Him first in our minds, hearts, and thoughts to give Him the priority due His holy name. The dishes can wait. The meal preparations can wait. Only one thing is needed, the thing that Mary chose. It's sitting at the feet of Jesus, listening to His voice.

"Just a Closer Walk with Thee"

A few years back the daughter of a close friend of mine was diagnosed with cancer. She fought bravely but slowly went downhill. My friend has an unlisted phone number, and whenever he phones me, his number doesn't show up on the caller ID.

One day I received a call from a number that didn't show up. I answered the call. The caller didn't say one word—not even hello. All I heard on the other end was the sound of crying, yet instantly I knew that it was my friend, and I knew that his daughter had just passed away.

I told him I loved him. I told him I was so sorry for the deep sorrow they were going through. And I prayed for him. All that time he never said one word. I'd known my friend for more than thirty years. I could hear his groaning, and I knew it was him and what had happened.

When I finished praying, he whispered, "Thank you," and then hung up.

I want to be really careful that I don't reduce the story of my friend's daughter to a mere anecdote. That is never my intention at all. She lived an example of a life of excellence, and her life was rich, deep, and full.

Yet the story of her father and me on the phone together reminds me of the sort of relationship God calls us to have with Him.

God wants us to recognize His voice through the closeness of the relationship He has with us. There may be times when God doesn't even use words to communicate with us. We can sense His emotion. Maybe He's grieved over a situation. Or maybe He's blessed by a situation. The invitation He holds out to us is to draw near to Him while He draws near to us (James 4:8). The gift He offers is a personal, ongoing, intimate relationship with Him.

In the garden of Eden, God spoke personally and daily with Adam and Eve. Immediately after they sinned, Adam became afraid of hearing God's voice and of interacting with Him. God was deeply grieved by this change in their relationship. But when Jesus died on the cross, He restored all that was lost in Eden, including our ability to personally talk with and hear God.

Like a close friend or a spouse, we learn to recognize God's voice by being with Him and by talking with Him often. God never intended for us to live by our consciences alone, by deciding what's good and evil or right and wrong. We were created to hear and respond to the voice of God.

I promise you this: when God is our highest priority, pursuit, and passion, we will recognize His voice.

And when we don't hear Him, then we just need to trust His silence.

CHAPTER NINE

HEAR GOD'S
VOICE FOR OTHERS

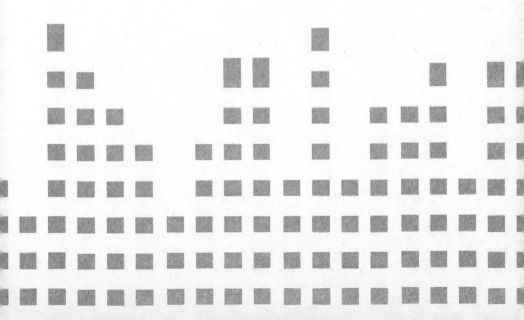

Pursue love, and desire spiritual gifts, but
especially that you may prophesy.
—1 Corinthians 14:1

One evening I was in a restaurant when a man and his wife came in, and I couldn't help but notice that the man was bodybuilder huge. I mean, this guy was ripped. He put Charles Atlas to shame. But what struck me the most about their entry into the restaurant was that as soon as they walked in, I heard the Lord speak to my spirit about them, and I knew I needed to go talk to these strangers about something the Lord wanted to convey to them.

Wow!

Have you ever found yourself in a similar situation? You sense that the Holy Spirit is speaking to you on another person's behalf. Maybe you wonder if you're truly hearing the voice of God. It feels weird to walk up to someone you don't know and say, "Hey, I've got a word from God for you." Maybe the person will laugh at you. Or—in the case of the bodybuilder—maybe punch you out. And you don't want to be presumptuous either or get in anybody's face. You don't want to be rude and walk up to someone and exclaim, "Thus saith the Lord! Repent!" You wonder if what you sensed in your spirit wasn't really from the Lord after all. Maybe you just ate a bad slice of pizza, and all you have is indigestion.

I've been in those situations before and ignored the feeling. But I had come to learn that if I ignored that feeling, then usually God wouldn't let up on me, and that's what hit me there in the restaurant that day. I remembered that if a nudge from the Holy Spirit was truly a nudge from the Holy Spirit, then the nudge wouldn't go away. So I prayed about the nudge and asked the Lord to confirm the feeling, and the nudge stayed. I'd had enough experience with the voice of God by then to know that if the nudge was in line with Scripture and it stayed, then I needed to act on the nudge.

My heart started beating faster. I waited until the couple was seated first, then walked up to them and said politely, "Hey, I don't want to bother you, but I have a question." The man nodded, so I continued, "I'm a really perceptive individual, and I was just wondering . . . have you ever lifted weights before?"

The couple laughed, and the man said, "Yeah, a couple of times."

So I turned serious and said, "I don't want to sound weird or anything, but I'm a Christian, and the real reason I came over to you is because I felt like the Lord told me to tell you something. Do you mind if I tell it to you?"

The man and his wife looked at each other, then back at me. They both nodded as an indication for me to go ahead.

I motioned to the man and continued, "In my mind I saw you as a little boy sitting in an older woman's lap. I think it was your grandmother. You were crying, and she had a Bible, and she told you the story of Samson. And she said to you, 'If you will live for the Lord, then God will make you as strong as Samson.' God wanted me to tell you that He's kept up His end of the deal, but you haven't kept up your end of the deal." (Now, when you tell something as strong as that to Mr. America, you need to be sure you heard from the Lord. And one way you can do that is by being a friend of God, as we talked about earlier in this book. When you talk to God all the time, and God talks to you, you learn to recognize His voice.)

Well, the man put his head down when I said that, and when he looked up again, he had tears in his eyes. "Would you like to sit down a moment?" he asked. "I want to tell you something." I sat down, and the man continued, "I was raised by my grandmother. My mother was a single mom, and she worked all the time. One day I was walking home from school, and these bigger boys threw rocks at me and called me names. One of the rocks hit me in the head and cut my head. When I got home, my grandmother held me in her lap, and I was crying. She was a strong believer. She got out her Bible and read me the story of Samson. She told me that if I would serve God, then God would make me strong, like Samson. I prayed, and I told God that I wanted that. Just a few minutes ago on the way to the restaurant, I told my wife that story for the first time. The reason I told her is that these days I have everything I've ever wanted. Money. Strength. A certain amount of fame. But I'm miserable. I told her that we need to find our way back to God. We need to get our lives straight. We need to start going back to church."

Right there at the restaurant table, I led the two of them to Christ.

The next Sunday they came to church with me.

I tell you that story because sometimes we will hear God's voice for the purpose of passing along a word to someone else. God could speak to the person directly, but maybe that person isn't in the habit of hearing God's voice, and if the word comes from someone else, then it actually comes with more power. Just like the situation of the couple in the restaurant, the circumstances are so striking that they can't be written off as a coincidence. People are more apt to listen to someone else. They're more likely to know that God is truly speaking to them.

You may have never heard that you can receive a word from the Lord to pass on to others, and if it sounds surprising, initially, or even shocking, that's okay. Pray that the Lord will open your heart to this matter because I don't want you to miss this important truth. If you're a believer, then God wants to speak to you. Sometimes what He says will be for your edification, and sometimes it will be for another person.

We call this experience of hearing God's voice for the sake of others *prophecy*. It's a gift that God gives to believers through the power of His Holy Spirit. And if you're in the habit of hearing God's voice, then this is a gift He gives to you.

Prophecy Is for You

Sometimes Christians get concerned when they hear the word *prophecy* because there have been abuses of the concept in times past—and there really is more than one way we can use the word today, so we need to carefully define it.

Maybe you're justifiably concerned because someone once walked up to you after a church service and said, "Hey, I've got a word from the Lord for you." But what he or she said was discouraging, disruptive, and weird, not in line with Scripture, and you're pretty sure that what the person told you wasn't from the Lord.

Or maybe you've read something or seen something on the news about how a smooth-tongued leader proclaimed himself to be a prophet of the Lord, and he issued some doomsday prediction about how the world was supposed to go up in smoke at a certain time and on a certain day—or about how Jesus was supposed to return at a certain time on a certain day, or how plagues would kill mankind, or how Martians would be coming down to earth in a spaceship to cart us all away. It was like the Y2K scare but with spiritual implications, and the prediction didn't come true. So now what?

In the strictest sense of the word, prophets in the Old Testament foretold the future, and God required in Scripture that 100 percent of everything a prophet spoke needed to come to pass. If it didn't—even if the prophet had a really high average, like nine out of ten—then the prophet was put to death as a false prophet, a hugely serious crime. That's a very stringent requirement. Absolutely everything a prophet predicted needed to happen, or else he was killed (Deut. 18:20–22)—end of story.

Similarly, in several places in the New Testament, we are warned about false prophets. So it's right to keep our guard up and to be discerning when people say they have a word from the Lord for us. These prophets might look good or sound good or do good things on the surface, but if what they're saying isn't in line with the gospel of Jesus Christ or the rest of Scripture, then we are to beware of them.

Jesus warned His followers about such people in Matthew 7:15, saying, "Beware of false prophets, who come to you in sheep's clothing, but inwardly they are ravenous wolves." Paul, in 2 Corinthians 11:13–14, compared the work of false prophets to the work of Satan, saying, "For such are false apostles, deceitful workers, transforming themselves into apostles of Christ. And no wonder! For Satan himself transforms himself into an angel of light." Paul issues another warning in Galatians 1:8, saying, "But even if we, or an angel from heaven, preach any other gospel to you than what we have preached to you, let him be accursed."

So we need to be wary of people who make predictions about the future, particularly if these predictions aren't in line with revealed Scripture. Jesus said four times in the New Testament that no one would know the day or the hour of the coming of the Lord.[1] That pretty much ends that discussion right there. And we need to make absolutely sure that anything a prophet says is in line with the gospel.

Yet let's put these abuses aside for a moment because the other way of using the word *prophecy*—the more general sense in which I'm using it—is biblical and something for us all to take note of. In the more general sense of the word, *prophecy* is an encouraging message from the Lord that we give someone. A prophet is someone who speaks and teaches the words of God. In this sense, a pastor or leader who opens his Bible and preaches from God's revealed word in Scripture is a prophet. In this sense also, a Christian who is prompted by the Holy Spirit to speak or act in a certain way has been given the gift of prophecy. (It has been explained, helpfully, that *prophecy* can mean either the foretelling or forth-telling of God's word.)

The Hebrew word for *prophet* used in the Old Testament is *nabi*. It means "one who announces."[2] It's a general, comprehensive word. In Genesis 20:7, Abraham was called a "prophet" (*nabi*), and even though we typically don't think of Abraham as a prophet, the Bible calls him one in this more general use of the word. He was a friend of God (James 2:23), and God spoke to him, and he passed along this teaching to others.

The Greek word for *prophet* used in the New Testament is *prophetes.* It means "God's spokesman," or "someone who speaks God's message for a particular situation."[3] Jesus is perceived to be a "prophet" by the woman at the well in John 4:19. The same word is used in 1 Corinthians 12:28, where "God has appointed these in the church: first apostles, second *prophets,* third teachers, after that miracles, then gifts of healings, helps, administrations, varieties of tongues."

Some scholars believe that the gift of prophecy has ended these days, but I don't see that from Scripture, particularly from the two passages I just mentioned and particularly if we take into consideration the wider view of the word and its gifting. Today's prophets are to speak the words of the Lord and instruct, comfort, encourage, rebuke, and convict. And when a prophet speaks in a church, Scripture is clear that his words are to be evaluated because his words are not on the same level as the inspired Scripture. First Corinthians 14:29 says, "Let two or three prophets speak, and let the others judge."

Other scholars believe that the gift of prophecy is the same today as the gift of teaching or preaching because the two gifts essentially accomplish the same task—helping others hear from God. And it's true that the gifts of preaching, teaching, and prophecy are very similar. But I'd say that a person could prophesy in church without necessarily bringing forth a sermon. And a person might be able to teach a Sunday school class, for instance, without ever speaking God's message for a particular situation. So there's still a case for a distinction to be made.

One other item of note is that Scripture is clear that prophets can be both men and women. In Acts 21:8–9, Philip the evangelist had four unmarried daughters who prophesied, and this function was considered blessed and welcomed by the early church.

So let's take a closer look at this gift of prophecy, this experience of hearing the voice of the Lord for the purpose of imparting His message to others. Here are three biblical distinctions that apply to us.

1. All Christians Can Hear God for the Edification of Others

When we receive the Holy Spirit—and as we yield our lives to Him, and He fills and influences our lives—He walks alongside us, encouraging us, guiding us, leading us, assuring us. He doesn't want to be silent. He wants to have an intimate, communicative relationship with us. As we walk with Him, He will speak to us and give us words or impressions that encourage others.

One slight difference needs to be made within this distinction. All Christians can prophesy, yet not every believer has the specific gift of prophecy. If that sounds contradictory, hang on, and I'll explain what I mean. God clearly doesn't give every spiritual gift to every believer. For instance, we know that not every Christian has the gift of administration because there are plenty of Christians who don't know beans about organization, supervision, or spiritual management. And that's okay because with different gifts we all learn to function together as a church. In 1 Corinthians 12:12–31, Paul paints a picture of believers having different gifts, just as a human body has different parts, yet all gifts function together for the sake of unity in the church. "The eye cannot say to the hand, 'I don't need you!' And the head cannot say to the feet, 'I don't need you!'" (v. 21 NIV). So there are clearly different gifts given to different believers, and not all believers have the same gifts.

What is the specific gift of prophecy? Paul, in Ephesians 4:11–12, describes it this way: "And He Himself gave some to be apostles, some prophets, some evangelists, and some pastors and teachers, for the equipping of the saints for the work of ministry, for the edifying of the body of Christ." The list in this passage spells out specific gifts given to believers to do the work of ministry. This verse is helpful because in it we can see this dual truth that not every believer has every specific gift, yet all believers are still called to walk in certain areas. For instance, not all believers will have the specific gift of being an evangelist even though all believers are called to evangelize others. Not all believers will have the specific gift of being a pastor even though all believers are called to shepherd others. Not all people will have the specific gift of prophecy even though all Christians nevertheless can hear God for the edification of others. So any Christian can give someone an encouraging message from the Lord, regardless of whether he or she has the specific gift of prophecy.

One of the foundational passages for us to consider here is Numbers 11. In this passage Moses had been doing too much of the work, leading the Israelites by himself, and he was tired and burned-out. He even prayed that God would kill him. But God said Moses had made a classic leadership mistake: he hadn't delegated. He tried to bear the burden alone. What Moses needed to do was select some elders who could help bear the burden and help lead the people along with him.

So Moses did that. With the Lord's guidance, Moses gathered seventy men, and the Spirit of the Lord rested on these men, and they helped Moses. "Then the LORD came down in the cloud, and spoke to him, and took of the Spirit that was upon him, and placed the same upon the seventy elders; and it happened, when the Spirit rested upon them, that they prophesied, although they never did so again" (v. 25).

We wouldn't classify these seventy elders as having a lifelong gift of prophecy, a gift they used regularly with many people they met. But they prophesied for a time. That's an example of people using a gift but not having it specifically.

We are all told to prophesy. Paul, in 1 Corinthians 14:1, reminds us to "pursue love, and desire spiritual gifts, but *especially that you may prophesy*." Why would Paul say to do that if not all believers could do it? Why would the Bible tell us to desire something that's only for a select few? The answer is that we all are to prophesy as the Lord allows it. He will bestow the specific gift on a few believers. And He will give the general ability to all believers.

Another foundational verse is Acts 2:17–18. Peter was preaching in Jerusalem, and he quoted the prophet Joel:

"And it shall come to pass in the last days, says God,
That I will pour out of My Spirit on all flesh;
Your sons and your daughters shall prophesy,
Your young men shall see visions,
Your old men shall dream dreams.
And on My menservants and on My maidservants
I will pour out My Spirit in those days;
And they shall prophesy."

Let me tell you, we're living in those last days. God has poured out His Spirit on us, and both men and women are able to prophesy, hear the word of the Lord, and pass along an encouraging message from God. In that sense, we all can prophesy. All Christians can hear God for the edification of others.

2. Prophecy Is Never Manipulative

Prophecy is never about getting others to do what we want them to do. It's far too easy to walk up to someone and say, "Hey, the Lord told me to say to you such and such," when we're only giving our opinion to the person, and then adding "thus saith the Lord" to strengthen our opinion.

Scripture holds forth strong warnings for those who misuse the name of God in this manner. In Jeremiah 23:25–26, God is quoted as saying, "I have heard what the prophets have said who prophesy lies in My name, saying, 'I have dreamed, I have dreamed!' How long will this be in the heart of the prophets who prophesy lies? Indeed they are prophets of the deceit of their own heart."

In verses 30–31, God adds, "'Therefore behold, I am against the prophets,' says the LORD, 'who steal My words every one from his neighbor. Behold, I am against the prophets,' says the LORD, 'who use their tongues and say, "He says."'"

That's clear. If we simply say any old thing that pops into mind and add, "That's what God says about the matter," then God says that is not right, and He warns us not to do it. An example of this action is given in Ezekiel 22:28. "Her prophets plastered them with untempered mortar, seeing false visions, and divining lies for them, saying, 'Thus says the Lord GOD,' when the LORD had not spoken."

One of the Ten Commandments, the third, says we are not to take the Lord's name in vain (Ex. 20:7). When we apply this teaching today, we tend to relegate the commandment only to forbidding the use of God's name as a curse word. Now, certainly I don't believe we should use God's name as a curse word, but I believe the commandment is broader than that. The word *vain* is closely associated with vanity. If a person is vain or has vanity, then it means the person is self-focused to the point of being selfish, even self-obsessed. With this definition in mind, to use the name of God in vain means to use God's name for selfish reasons. It means we use God's name with our wills at the forefront. We use God's name for selfish motives.

A friend saw an incident develop at his church when an older single man approached a younger single woman and told her that he'd received a word from the Lord for her. The woman asked what the word was. The older man said that the Lord had told him to tell her that she was to marry him and bear him many children. The older man and the younger woman were not dating and hardly knew each other. When the woman protested, the man insisted and wouldn't take no for an answer. He began driving by her apartment and phoning her at all hours, leaving messages that she needed to obey the Lord. Finally the woman brought the matter to the church elders, who confronted the man and told him to back off. In the all-important matter of marriage, the Lord will certainly guide, yet the Lord needs to speak to both parties, and if the woman's answer was no, then it was no. What this man was doing wasn't acting in prophecy; it was simple harassment.

One important factor about words from the Lord needs always to be considered: confirmation. If a person has a word from the Lord for you, then God will confirm it in your own spirit. He won't leave you out of the matter. We've already discussed how God is a friend, and God as a friend would never tell somebody something important about your life without also telling it to you. First Corinthians 14:32–33 says, "And the spirits of the prophets are subject to the prophets. For God is not the author of confusion but of peace, as in all the churches of the saints."

My staff at church knows that I pray extensively about what to preach on each weekend. In fact, when people approach me and say, "Hey, Pastor Robert, will you preach a series on this?" I say to them, "I'd love to, but you need to talk to my Boss first because I don't set the topic for preaching. He does."

I received a call from one of our elders once, and he said, "Hey, Pastor Robert, I was praying for you this morning, and I got a strong impression from the Holy Spirit about what you should preach on next. I understand that God speaks to you about these matters, but this was so strong I felt like I ought to call you. The Holy Spirit indicated to me that in January you might preach a series on this." And he named the topic.

For a minute I thought the man was pulling my leg because I'd just walked out of the conference room with our media team, advising that I was going to preach on that exact topic the following month. I asked him, "Were you just at the church offices? Did you just talk with some-one?" He said he had not.

That's confirmation.

3. Prophecy Is Encouraging

God is concerned about our motives and attitude when we share with people. Prophecy builds people up. It doesn't tear people down. First Corinthians 14:3 is a foundational verse in this matter. "He who prophesies speaks edification and exhortation and comfort to men."

Prophecy is meant to encourage people—and every word spoken needs to line up with the Bible. The word *encourage* comes from the root word *courage* with the prefix *en*, which in English means "to put in." So a word of encouragement means you are to put courage into people. Don't put fear into people. It's very simple.

First Corinthians 14:31 augments this teaching: "For you can all prophesy one by one, that all may learn and all may be encouraged." Prophecy is so all may learn the words and intentions of God. When we prophesy, we are to share God's word with other people so they'll be encouraged. Even when I was telling that bodybuilder that he hadn't kept up his part of the bargain in walking with the Lord, I was doing it in an encouraging manner. I wasn't condemning the man. I was affirming the decision he'd already made, exhorting him to walk in a manner worthy of the Lord.

A famous leader in the Bible is Barnabas. Acts 4:36–37 mentions how he got his name: "And Joses, who was also named Barnabas by the apostles (which is translated Son of Encouragement), a Levite of the country of Cyprus, having land, sold it, and brought the money and laid it at the apostles' feet."

So here was this man named Joses whom everybody calls Son of Encouragement, and one of the first things we read about him is that he sold land and gave it to the apostles. That's a pretty encouraging action right there, not a selfish one. Then in Acts 11:22–23, we read more about how his name and his actions correspond: "Then news of these things came to the ears of the church in Jerusalem, and they sent out Barnabas to go as far as Antioch. When he came and had seen the grace of God, he was glad, and encouraged them all that with purpose of heart they should continue with the Lord."

That's a powerful verse because it says when Barnabas came and saw the church in Antioch, he saw a lot of grace. Romans tells us where sin abounds, grace abounds all the more. So Barnabas could have focused on their sins, but he chose to focus on the work of God in their lives, on grace. He encouraged them to continue with the Lord.

Acts 15:30–32 continues this thought: "So when they were sent off, they came to Antioch; and when they had gathered the multitude together, they delivered the letter. When they had read it, they rejoiced over its encouragement. Now Judas and Silas, themselves being prophets also, exhorted and strengthened the brethren with many words." The text doesn't say that the apostles corrected, rebuked, and tore the church down. It says they exhorted and strengthened the brethren. That's the ministry of prophecy.

How many times have you thought to call someone or send someone a note or a card and just encourage this person? It's very possible that you're already hearing God because where did that thought come from? It didn't come from the Devil. Every time you have a thought to encourage someone in the Lord, you're hearing God.

One morning, a few years back, in August, I had a very specific dream about a friend of mine, a pastor in another state. The dream was so strong that I remembered it vividly when I woke. I got up and dressed to go walking, normally the first thing I do each morning. As I walked, I prayed for my friend, and God kept impressing upon me the need to pray for my friend. Normally on my walks I pray for the church, my kids, my wife, my other friends, and all sorts of things. But that day I spent my whole time in prayer for my friend. I wasn't sure what I should pray for; I just prayed that God would encourage my friend and strengthen him.

Well, life got busy as it so often does, and after my walk I didn't think to call my friend. But a few weeks later he came to mind again, so I called him. I told him about the dream and about praying for him, and we talked for a while. It turned out that his father had passed away. It was the very day I'd had the dream about my friend and prayed for him. My friend said that although the day of his father's passing had been sad, my friend had felt people praying for him that day, and he was greatly encouraged because of that.

A Word from the Lord Can Change Everything

Pastor Alec Rowlands, in his helpful book *The Presence*, tells of a time when he heard a word from the Lord through another person. It happened fairly early on in his ministry at Westgate Chapel in Seattle, the largest city in the Pacific Northwest, one of the least-churched regions of America. Alec and his wife, Rita, had been at the church for four years, and the honeymoon of the recruitment phase was over, and discouragement and frustration had set in.

The church seemed caught in a rut. Alec had preached about prayer and had constantly emphasized the necessity and wonderment of being in the presence of God, but the response from the congregation seemed unenthusiastic, even stifled. About thirteen hundred people attended the church in those days, but only about thirty people could be coaxed to come out to each midweek prayer meeting.

One sleepy summer Sunday during the 9:00 a.m. service, everything seemed to go off as planned. The congregation sang some songs of worship. Alec introduced a visiting missionary. The offering was given. Alec delivered the sermon. The Sunday seemed like any other Sunday. The 11:00 a.m. service began the same way. But then something changed.

Right after the worship portion of the service, one man in the balcony remained standing. Alec knew him to be a godly man. He and his family had been involved at the church for several years, and the man was in community with other godly believers at the church and demonstrably under the authority of the church leadership. Alec knew him to be a man of prayer with a tremendous heart for worship.

The man began speaking from the balcony. Having unplanned speeches such as this wasn't a regular occurrence at Westlake, although it had happened every now and again. The man wasn't speaking frantically or ecstatically, so Alec let it continue. The man simply spoke with reference to Luke 8:4–12, about how various "soils" were present in the congregation, meaning that people were spiritually receptive in different capacities. The man spoke of God's word breaking through, and he encouraged the congregation that the receptive soil would find reason to rejoice, and God would bring forth fruit from the word planted in good soil. Then the man sat down.

Alec described what he saw:

When the man sat down, I looked out across the congregation—and to this day what I saw I find hard to explain. Most in the congregation, main floor and balcony, were weeping. Some spontaneously gathered into small groups across the sanctuary and began to pray. Some stood to their feet, eyes closed, faces directed to heaven. Others lifted their hands before God, like a toddler reaching for a parent's love. Several hundred headed out of their seats for the altar area where they knelt to pray. No one had given any directive from the pulpit. I was concerned that anything I might do or say would disrupt the work God was so obviously doing. After a long while I went to the microphone and said, "God's not done, and we're not going to interfere with what he's doing. Please just keep your hearts open and surrendered to him." I sat down.

For the next forty-five minutes God took charge. I didn't preach. I didn't introduce the missionaries. The soloist didn't sing. We didn't take an offering. We all just went to prayer. Finally, when those who had been in the altar area headed back to their seats, I went to the microphone and gave an altar call for those who had never given their lives to Christ. Twenty-five people came forward. That service was normally over at 12:30. By one o'clock the sanctuary was still full. Nobody wanted to leave. By two o'clock it was still more than half full. The people continued in quiet prayer and worship. God's Presence broke through in an unusual way that day.

With the board's backing, the next Sunday we called for a solemn assembly to take place at the church the following Wednesday night [prayer meeting]. Based on my track record I remember thinking I'd be happy if a hundred people showed up. You can imagine my surprise that Wednesday night, when I walked out of my study into the sanctuary to find the main floor and balcony of our church packed. It was such a confirmation for me that this was a God-thing.[4]

More than twenty years later Alec described how that word from the Lord through the man in the balcony acted as the turning point for the entire church. Everything changed after that. Prayer changed. Worship changed. The atmosphere in the congregation changed. The staff changed. From that point onward to this day, an emphasis on prayer remains a constant in that church.

My friends, the Holy Spirit walks alongside us. He dwells within us, guiding us into all truth. He doesn't want to be silent; He wants to have an intimate, communicative relationship with us. As we walk with Him, He will speak to us and give us words, and sometimes these words will be for us. And at other times those words will be for the edification of others. Prophecy is never to be manipulative or used for selfish gain. It's another confirmation that God is at work in our midst.

My prayer for all of us is that we would learn to hear God's voice clearly and then act with confidence upon the impressions from the Holy Spirit that we receive. Let us all become gracious sons and daughters of encouragement for His name's sake. Amen.

CHAPTER TEN

HEAR GOD'S VOICE
FOR A BREAKTHROUGH

Thus also faith by itself, if it does not have works, is dead.
—James 2:17

I mentioned that Gateway is a multisite church of approximately thirty thousand weekly attendees. We currently have more than seven hundred people on staff, and I confess that I don't know all of our staff members personally although all of them are valuable to me, and I'm glad they're on board.

One of our staff members—I'll call her "Helen" (although that's not her real name)—serves as an administrative assistant. She and her husband have two small children, and the family was going through some difficult times financially. The children had outgrown their clothes, and Helen didn't know where the money would come from to buy new clothes for them. (The church pays competitive wages—don't worry. The problem arose from some unexpected bills that had come their way.) She needed a financial breakthrough.

At first, Helen thought it would be prudent to box up her children's clothes and take them to the consignment store to see if she could make a little extra money. But the morning she was set to do this, during her quiet time, she distinctly heard the voice of the Lord in her heart. *Step out in faith*, God said. *Give these clothes away to another young mother who needs them, and give them away first. Don't worry. Trust Me in this. For this very day, I will take care of the money you need for new clothes for your children.*

It was such a clear word, Helen said. She did exactly that. On her way to work that morning, she took the clothes to a young mother and gave them away. She then prayerfully waited with arms open wide in worship. (This is picture language I'm using to describe the worship that took place in her soul.) Helen went about her regular day at the office. She didn't say anything to anybody. She prayed in her spirit, and she worshipped in her heart, and she believed that God would provide for her and that God would do so that very day.

Here's the fun part of this story. A few months earlier I'd distinctly heard the voice of the Lord too. *I want you to give bonuses to the administrative assistants at Gateway, Robert.*

So I did. I arranged for bonuses through our compensation committee and eldership. This takes a while. The normal procedure is that a notice such as this would go through our associate staff members and pastors, who are the direct supervisors of the administrative assistants. The associate staff would actually relay the messages.

Yet here's another fun part of this story. My son is on staff at Gateway, and Helen works in his department. My son was scheduled to teach at a conference that day (the same day Helen had heard from the Lord), which meant he wouldn't be coming in to the office. But somehow he, too, felt led by the Spirit to do something particular. It was to drop by the office before he went to the conference. There in his in-box was the note about the bonuses for the administrative assistants. My son delivered the note to Helen the same day she heard from the Lord. Before the day was over, Helen knew the extra money was there. The timing was perfect. Helen had stepped out in faith, and God had provided.

I believe every Christian longs for similar breakthroughs from God. We long to hear God's voice clearly. We want God to speak to us regarding some area of concern.

Maybe we're praying for more faith. We long for a breakthrough so that having a quiet time is no longer a struggle. Or we want fresh perspective and spiritual understanding about a difficult time or event in our lives.

Maybe we're praying for our family; we want a closer relationship. Or we're praying for wayward children. Or maybe we're single and longing for a spouse.

Perhaps we're praying for a breakthrough in our finances. We long to either manage our money better or to make more money and not need to struggle so much anymore—either way, we long to hear God's voice in this area.

Perhaps we're praying for freedom in some area of our life where there's a stronghold or bondage. We want to get free from anger, bitterness, resentment, or lust.

Maybe we long for a breakthrough at work or in a friendship.

Picture it this way: many of us at some time have used a power drill to bore through a piece of wood. We're drilling and pushing, and we need to put pressure on it, and then suddenly the drill breaks through the other side of the board, and there's no resistance anymore. That's what God can do in every area of our lives. God breaks through a problem or situation to get us into the place of insight and understanding, faith, hope, or resolve. Sometimes a problem is solved, or sometimes it isn't, but the problem no longer has the same weight as before. A load is made easy, and a burden is made light. A new opportunity comes our way. A solution is at hand. A door is opened. A path forward is made clear.

Would you like a breakthrough in some area of your life that's been difficult? In this area, you've needed to push and struggle, and you've encountered resistance, but now there's hope ahead. God invites us to hear His voice for a breakthrough. Let's remind ourselves that hearing His voice for a breakthrough is certainly not a slot-machine process. We don't stick in a coin and out pops an answer. It's a relational process, a friendship process, a King-and-His-bondservant process, a Parent-and-His-heir process, a Lover-and-His-beloved process.

Are you longing for a breakthrough?

God invites you to a closer walk with Him. That's where your breakthrough will be found.

The Master of Breakthroughs

I love the story in 1 Chronicles 14, where David had been anointed king over Israel. As soon as that happened, "all the Philistines went up to search for David" (v. 8). That's not the part of the story I love. It meant that enemies were now after King David, and the lesson there is that as soon as the Enemy hears that something good has happened in your life, he comes against you. We don't need to be afraid of this opposition.[1] We have Christ, and greater is He who is in us than he who is in the world (1 John 4:4).

What I love in the story is David's response. The Bible says that David "heard of it and went out against them" (1 Chron. 14:8). The Philistines raided the valley of Rephaim first. "And David inquired of God, saying, 'Shall I go up against the Philistines? Will You deliver them into my hand?'" (v. 10)—meaning, shall I confront them in battle? Essentially, the first thing David did was talk with God. In the midst of his need for a breakthrough (this one against his enemies), David inquired of the Lord and asked to hear the Lord's voice about a specific matter.

That's the key to practicing faith. There's a famous verse that says, "So then faith comes by hearing, and hearing by the word of God" (Rom. 10:17). Of course, we already have the revealed Word of God—sixty-six books of revealed Word. Do we want to hear the Word of God? Then we need to open our Bibles and read. But as we've discussed throughout this book, sometimes we want a specific word from God too. We have the Bible, and we're already reading the Bible, but God is being silent on an issue about which the Bible doesn't speak directly. We wonder then how to act. What do we do? Which direction do we turn? What decision do we make? It's at such a time that we're invited to ask God to speak to us specifically. We long to hear God's voice. Sometimes God will speak to us by using a specific portion of Scripture, pointing our attention to it. Sometimes God will speak to our hearts by a nudging, an inclination. This is harder to quantify, yet it is God speaking nevertheless.

A friend and his wife received a call at three in the morning. Friends of theirs were having a baby, and he was particularly close to the husband, so my friend got up and got ready to go down to the hospital. As he was running around gathering this and that, he thought to himself, *Which car should I drive?* See, he had a car that he owned personally, and he had a different car that his company owned. He was the owner of the company, and he typically drove the company car to and from work. But he didn't know exactly how long he'd be at the hospital. If he drove to the hospital and from there to work, then the company car would be the one to take. But if he drove home first, then he knew he should take his personal car.

In the midst of all that frenzy, the Lord spoke to him and said, *Why don't you ask Me which car to take?*

So he said okay, sat down, and prayed. His wife asked him what he was doing because he'd been rushing around, and he said, "I believe I'm supposed to pray about which car to take."

In prayer, the man sensed the Lord distinctly saying, *Take the company car.*

So my friend got in his company car. He was on Interstate 635 in Dallas, driving about 65 miles an hour when a drunk driver going over 100 miles per hour flew up from behind and crashed into him. My friend's vehicle was completely totaled, and his back badly injured. He was unable to work for a while. There were a lot of medical expenses, and he lost contracts at work.

It turned out that the person who hit him had an insurance policy that paid out a maximum of $25,000. The personal car that my friend had left at home also had a $25,000 limit. But his company car had a coverage limit of $1 million—enough to pay for the medical expenses and lost wages. Listen—that prayer at three in the morning was a $975,000 prayer.

We can wonder why God didn't simply stop the accident, but God has fuller plans that we often don't see. The point is that my friend stopped to listen to God, and then he obeyed.

Similarly, God responded to David specifically. God told David to go up and engage in battle, for He would deliver the Philistines into David's hand (1 Chron. 14:10). That's the crux of the story because at that point David had a word from the Lord. He had exactly what he needed to act in faith. If we define faith as taking God at His word, then we need to have a word from God that we can believe in and act upon. Faith is never to be flung out into a void; faith must have God's word to stand on. David had asked God, and God had answered him. Once God tells us what to do, then we're not moving on presumption. We don't need to dream up faith or make it up or conjure it up. If we ask God, and God answers by His word, then we can have faith and act upon that word.

Note that the Bible says the Philistines raided the valley of Rephaim first. *Rephaim* means "giants."[2] The Philistines were trying to send a message to David. They were using straightforward scare tactics. They wanted to intimidate him. David could have responded with over-confidence. He might have thought, *Hey, I've killed giants before, and this is no big deal.* Or he could have responded with fear. *Man, these Philistines are something else. A nation of giants camping in the valley of giants.* But he did neither. Instead, his response was to inquire of the Lord. Why is this particularly significant?

Think this out with me. It is significant because David was no wimpy king. He was an experienced combat warrior by this point in his life. Sometimes when we read about David in Scripture, we picture him as a little boy with a slingshot. But that's a wrong picture through and through. Scripture describes how David killed a lion and a bear when he was a boy, and he didn't do it from a distance either. On more than one occasion he hiked after huge predatory animals, struck the animals, and delivered lambs from their mouths. When a lion or bear rose against him, David caught it by its head and killed it (1 Sam. 17:34–36). David must have been one tough kid. And by the time he was an adult, David must have looked like Conan the Barbarian. He was big, and he was bad. How much of a warrior was he? Here's another telling incident. When David was a young man, he liked the king's daughter, Michal. Her father told David that he could marry Michal, but first David had to kill one hundred enemy soldiers. That got David a little upset, so he went out, picked a fight, and killed two hundred enemy soldiers, twice as many as required (1 Sam. 18:25–27). This tells us clearly that David was a mighty warrior, probably without rival.

So why did David inquire of the Lord when the enemy was in the valley of Rephaim? David wanted to know that his initiative wouldn't be done on his own undertaking. David had strength and skill on his side—but he wanted to have faith too. Sure, he could have fought the Philistines by his own strength and skill alone. But David knew that a much greater strength and confidence would come from relying on God.

Can you imagine the scene? David's soldiers were all prepared for battle, but first they saw their king walk away and spend some time on his knees. The older soldiers might have nudged the younger soldiers with a knowing look. "That's your king in his strategy session," they'd say. "When he comes back, he'll have a word from God. We're going to win this thing. You'll see."

How does this relate to you and me? We will not have breakthroughs in our own lives unless we have faith. And we will not have faith unless we hear God. So we will not have any breakthroughs unless we purposely and regularly set aside time to hear from God. Faith is not a blind leap. The Bible says that God's word is a lamp to our feet and a light to our paths (Ps. 119:105). When God gives us a word, we have enough light to take the next step. Faith is never blind. Faith always relies upon God's Word—His directly inspired and flawless word written in the

Bible—and His word in specific situations spoken directly to our hearts. Once we hear God, then we can have true faith.

Here's what the outcome of the battle looked like:

> So they went up to Baal Perazim, and David defeated them there. Then David said, "God has broken through my enemies by my hand like a breakthrough of water." Therefore they called the name of that place Baal Perazim. And when they left their gods there, David gave a commandment, and they were burned with fire. (1 Chron. 14:11–12)

I prayed and studied over this passage on and off for two months before I caught the full significance of it. First Chronicles 14 tells the story, but it's also repeated in 2 Samuel 5:17–21, with one little twist:

> Now when the Philistines heard that they had anointed David king over Israel, all the Philistines went up to search for David. And David heard of it and went down to the stronghold. The Philistines also went and deployed themselves in the Valley of Rephaim. So David inquired of the LORD, saying, "Shall I go up against the Philistines? Will You deliver them into my hand?"
>
> And the LORD said to David, "Go up, for I will doubtless deliver the Philistines into your hand."
>
> So David went to Baal Perazim, and David defeated them there; and he said, "The LORD has broken through my enemies before me, like a breakthrough of water." Therefore he called the name of that place Baal Perazim. And they left their images there, and David and his men carried them away.

Do you see the twist? In 2 Samuel, David is specifically noted as calling the place Baal Perazim—and that bothered me at first. Baal was the name of the Philistine's false god, and Baal Perazim means "master of breakthroughs."³ So why would David call it that? At first glance it almost sounds as though David is calling Baal the master of breakthroughs.

But here's what I found. This particular mountain was named Mount Baal before this battle. The enemy had a temple there, and the Philistines stored a lot of their idols at the temple. This was the place where the enemy felt strongest and surest. There's no doubt in my mind that David credits the victory to Jehovah because earlier in 1 Chronicles 14, he says, "God has broken through my enemies by my hand like a breakthrough of water" (v. 11). Also notice that one of the first things David did after the battle was destroy the enemy's idols, either by burning them with fire or carting them away, probably both. So this is key: David wasn't saying that Baal was the master of breakthroughs. David was saying that Baal was broken through. Baal was defeated. The false idols were destroyed. David wanted everyone after that to know that the site of the pagan temple was the same site where Baal was done away with.

Here's our application. The place in our lives where the Enemy thinks he's the strongest is the exact place where God desires to give us breakthroughs. Is there one area of your life where you've never been able to gain victory? This place can be a Baal Perazim kind of place, a place where the Enemy is soundly defeated. God is the master of breakthroughs. God will give you a victory in the exact area where you don't think you can have a breakthrough. What's required is faith.

Pray and Obey

But faith is not enough.

Does that statement shock you? We need to be extremely careful here. Our salvation always comes by grace through faith alone, not by works so no one can boast (Eph. 2:8–9). Yet if we want a breakthrough, we need faith plus something else. Do you know what the something else is?

It's works.

James 2:17 says, "Thus also faith by itself, if it does not have works, is dead." If we have faith but that's all we have, then the Bible indicates that our faith is dead. Nothing is going to happen. A person can go around all day saying, "Oh, yes, I believe in God. I hear from the Lord all the time. I read the Bible every day. I know what's in Scripture. I believe, I believe, I believe." But if all he has is belief, then the Bible indicates that this is nothing. Even the demons believe in God (James 2:19). So we need to put action to our faith for our faith to amount to anything. Good works are the expression of our faith; indeed, "we are God's handiwork, created in Christ Jesus to do good works" (Eph. 2:10 NIV).

When a friend of mine was in college, he applied to work at a Christian camp one summer. He knew camps can be tremendous harvest fields for the kingdom of God. Now, if you're a young person and you've never worked at a camp, I highly recommend the experience. You will gain in one summer the experience and growth that it normally takes a full year in school to gain.

So my friend applied in January to work at this camp, and he really believed that God wanted him there. But in the spring of that year he became sick. Each morning for several weeks on end, he threw up. He went to doctors and finally got to the root of the problem and got some medicine, but the doctors said the medicine would take a while to kick in, and that they might actually need to try a couple of different medicines before one worked. So now my friend had a decision to make. Should he still work at this camp or not? Camp takes a lot of physical energy, and my friend knew he didn't have much to give.

College was finished for the year, and my friend went home to his parents' house for two weeks before camp started. He contacted the camp director and filled him in on the situation. The director wisely told him to pray about it, so my friend did. He prayed every day for two weeks that God would give him a specific word about whether to go to camp or not. He was still feeling sick during this time.

One verse that stuck out to him was 1 Peter 5:2, where Peter exhorts young Christian leaders, "Be shepherds of God's flock that is under your care . . . not because you must, but because you are willing" (NIV). He knew that God wasn't forcing him to go to camp. But my friend was definitely willing to go there. He wanted to be a part of this important shepherding ministry. Still, he sought to hear God's voice more closely on this matter.

The clock was ticking. He needed to give the camp director a final word by four o'clock Tuesday afternoon, when they were next scheduled to speak. So my friend specifically prayed that God would speak to him before that date and time. Each day he prayed and prayed but received silence. Then, at five minutes before four o'clock on Tuesday, my friend was lying on his bed, still feeling nauseated. He was praying specifically whether God wanted him at this place of harvest, and he read Micah 4:13, "Rise and thresh" (NIV).

These were three important words. Immediately the Lord impressed upon his heart that he was indeed to go to camp. He was to rise up off his sickbed and go to this ministry to thresh the spiritual harvest. He was to step forward in faith, believe God had spoken, take Him at His word, and undertake this ministry.

Even with that specific word from the Lord, do you know what still needed to take place? My friend still needed to act. He had faith, and now he needed to do something about it. And he did. Even though he was still feeling sick, my friend phoned the camp director that same hour and told him that he would come to camp. Then the next day he loaded up his old car and drove five hours to the camp's location. Beyond prayer, he still needed to move in the direction that he believed God wanted him to go.

The good news with this story is that within one week of being at camp, my friend stopped feeling sick. His stomach healed up, he felt fine from then on, and that summer turned out to be a wonderful experience where many young people were brought closer to Jesus.

The same action was required of King David, just as it's required for you and me—faith and works, prayer and obedience. Right after David destroyed the Philistine idols, the Philistines came back for another fight. First Chronicles 14:13–17 picks up the story:

> Then the Philistines once again made a raid on the valley. Therefore David inquired again of God, and God said to him, "You shall not go up after them; circle around them, and come upon them in front of the mulberry trees. And it shall be, when you hear a sound of marching in the tops of the mulberry trees, then you shall go out to battle, for God has gone out before you to strike the camp of the Philistines." So David did as God commanded him, and they drove back the army of the Philistines from Gibeon as far as Gezer. Then the fame of David went out into all lands, and the LORD brought the fear of him upon all nations.

It's a strange word from the Lord, isn't it? "When you hear a sound of marching in the tops of the mulberry trees . . . go out to battle" (v. 15). I can't imagine that sound; can you? And it must have come as a surprise to David's generals when he relayed to them what he'd heard from God. Remember: they'd just attacked the Philistines and won. But now they were not to attack the same way again. The word from the Lord was to go by a grove of mulberry trees and listen for the sound of marching in the leaves. That was the signal to attack. I can picture some of the soldiers scratching their heads and saying, "Well, it's not the most conventional way to win a battle. But let's give it a shot."

See, it took not only faith—it took action. David heard from the

Lord, and then he needed to put that hearing into practice. Let me give you another definition of action or works: obedience.

In other words, when we hear God saying something to us, we need to obey. When we inquire of the Lord and He directs our paths straight, then we need to run in the direction of those straight paths. A simple definition of *obedience* is doing what God says. Obey what you hear God telling you to do.

In Matthew 7:24–27, Jesus is preaching the Sermon on the Mount, and He says this:

> "Therefore whoever hears these sayings of Mine, and does them, I will liken him to a wise man who built his house on the rock: and the rain descended, the floods came, and the winds blew and beat on that house; and it did not fall, for it was founded on the rock.
>
> "But everyone who hears these sayings of Mine, and does not do them, will be like a foolish man who built his house on the sand: and the rain descended, the floods came, and the winds blew and beat on that house; and it fell. And great was its fall."

This wise man heard the voice of God and obeyed Him.

The foolish man also heard the voice of God. But the foolish man did whatever he felt like doing. He built his house on sand. Floods came, winds blew, and the house fell down.

Faith requires action, and it must be the action of obedience. If you want a breakthrough in your finances, then God invites you to do more than pray about getting out of debt. He wants you to tithe, spend only within your limits, manage your money, and get on a budget. You've got to align yourself with the direction God wants you to go and then walk down that path.

If you want a breakthrough in your family, God invites you to purposely set aside time to invest in each member. Work to communicate, to listen and be understood. Be gracious. Forgive. Love boldly. Don't walk away.

If you want a breakthrough in an addiction, God invites you to do whatever it takes to walk in the path of freedom. Be willing to be inconvenienced. Be willing to set aside the pleasures of sin. Pray for deliverance. Align yourself with God's good plan for your life.

Faith and works.

Listen and obey.

The Relief of Trusting God

A while back, just after my niece Erin graduated from college, she was working at a job she absolutely hated. It was a negative work environment where many of the workers were unhappy, and that attitude has a way of being contagious. Erin felt frustrated with her job, and she didn't know what to do about it. She felt that the Lord was holding out on her—that somehow she'd gotten shortchanged by God.

Erin came to a women's conference that we hold every year at Gateway. She prayed that God would show her if she should stay at her job or leave. If she was to leave, where was she supposed to go? What Erin longed for was a breakthrough.

Here's the rest of the story in her own words:

I came to the conference really wanting to hear from the Lord. I remember praying for God's voice. I was thinking that maybe God wanted me to stay at that job because He wanted me to be a witness there. But about halfway through the conference, God broke through and indicated that something else was going on. The Lord was allowing me to be in that job because it was a strategic experience in my life. Working at this job was actually a gift that God was giving me. It was an opportunity if I chose to embrace it. God was developing vital things within me.

At the conference, we were in a session where the speaker was talking about how, normally, it takes only about eleven days to walk the distance from Egypt to the promised land. But it took the Israelites forty years to go the same distance. Why? Because of the hardness of their hearts. They chose not to obey God. So I knew that ahead of me, I could either have an eleven-day or a forty-year journey. A lot of that would depend on how I responded to God's voice.

I kept praying about what I should do about my job, and God said,

I'm not going to tell you that, Erin, but I am going to tell you what I want you to do this upcoming Monday. When you go back to work, I want you to change your attitude. I want you to change the way you think about things. I want you to know that I place you in certain experiences for a reason. I am a good God, and I always have a purpose for everything. So I want you to go from feeling beat down and shortchanged and disappointed to believing and acting like you know I'm good and that I have a purpose for everything. Even this.

I left the conference on Saturday, feeling excited that I'd heard from the Lord. Now I needed to lean into that. I needed to change my way of thinking by Monday. I decided to trust the Lord—and act on that trust too. There was definitely a sense where God said,

Erin, you asked me for a word, and I've given it to you. So now what are you going to do about it? Your response to what I've told you is going to determine how long you spend in this stage of life. I've given you the word you've asked for. Now you need to follow through and do the things I told you to do.

Sure, there was a reality where I hated the job and was miserable, but there was also another reality where, by trusting in God, I could change my expectations and decide to be positive about my life and circumstances, knowing that God loves us and takes care of us and works all things together for our good.

And things did change. I saw how God was developing gratitude and perspective within me, character traits that I might not ever have had unless I'd gone through this dark experience.

It was not even two months later when the Lord released me from that job, and I had four job offers within a week. I took one of those jobs and am in that job today, and it's the best of the best.

And I know that God's timing was perfect. I was in my first job for a year and a half. Everybody around me was telling me I needed to get out of that job, but I didn't feel released by the Lord. I can see now that if I'd jumped ship then, I would have missed out on a great opportunity that God had in store for me at just the right time because the wonderful job I'm in right now was not available until the right time.

I see a similar pattern with a lot of my friends with their jobs. They're unhappy, and they might even feel shortchanged by God, that somehow God is holding out on them. But the truth is that God loves you, and He's got you where He's got you for a reason. The more you start listening to God's voice, looking for that reason, and trying to understand it, instead of pouting about it, the faster you're going to get the value out of it because there is value to it. There's a reason for it.

Friends, our lives are filled with constant noises competing for our attention. Yet many of us will never hear the one voice we most long to hear. In the midst of all the noise in our lives, God is speaking. Do we hear Him? And when we hear Him, do we obey?

Hearing God is what distinguishes our lives as believers. Because we have a personal relationship with God, we can hear His voice. If you are longing for a breakthrough today, then I encourage you to thank the Lord that He has given you the ability to communicate with Him spiritually. Thank Him that He wants to speak to you. God is always good. He always loves us. Ask Him to help you learn to recognize His voice and follow His leading. Commit yourself to listen to Him. And then obey His voice. Praise Him for giving you the opportunity to interact with Him—the Creator of the universe.

I'm so grateful that our God is a speaking God. I'm so grateful that He didn't lose His voice two thousand years ago. I'm so grateful that God doesn't change (Mal. 3:6). I'm so grateful that Jesus is the same yesterday, today, and forever (Heb. 13:8). I'm so grateful that He desires to have an intimate, ongoing, passionate, and vital relationship with us. I'm so grateful that our God desires to hear us and talk to us. Jesus said it very clearly in John 10:27, "My sheep hear My voice, and I know them, and they follow Me."

We can hear our Shepherd's voice. We can hear God. Amen.

A PRAYER TO
HEAR GOD'S VOICE

O Father God, I begin by worshipping You. I say with the psalmist that the heavens declare Your glory, God, and the skies show Your handiwork. You are mighty, and You are due strength and adoration and glory. I worship You, Lord, in the beauty of Your holiness. You reign, and I praise Your great and awesome name, for You are holy. You love justice. You are righteous. I exalt You, Lord, and I worship at Your footstool. You are great. You are always good. Amen.

Jesus, God has highly exalted You and bestowed on You the name that is above every name, so that at the name of Jesus, every knee should bow, in heaven and on earth and under the earth, and every tongue confess that Jesus Christ is Lord. Worthy are You, our Lord and God, to receive glory and honor and power, for You created all things, and by Your will they exist and were created. Amen.

O Holy Spirit, You are eternal. Your presence is everywhere, and Your hand leads us, and Your right hand holds us. You search all things, even the deep things of God, and You reveal these things to those who love You. You are our helper, Holy

Spirit, and the Father sent You to us in Jesus' name, saying that You will teach us all things and bring to remembrance all things that Jesus said. Amen.

O God, I confess to You my sins. You are faithful and just to forgive and cleanse me from all unrighteousness. Let the words of my mouth and the meditation of my heart be acceptable in Your sight, O Lord, my strength and my redeemer. You promise that though our sins are like scarlet, they shall be white as snow. Amen.

Help me always, by Your mercies, to present myself as a living sacrifice, holy and acceptable to You, which is my spiritual act of worship. O Lord, I do not want to be conformed to this world, but I want to be transformed by the renewal of my mind, that by testing I may discern what is the will of God, what is good and acceptable and perfect. Amen.

O Lord, I am reminded in Scripture that You invite us to draw near to You, and that You will draw near to us. I enter Your gates with thanksgiving and Your courts with praise. I give thanks to You and bless Your name. Amen.

Lord, Your Word tells us that You bring out Your own sheep, and You go before them, and the sheep follow You, for they know Your voice. Help me to hear and know Your voice, O Lord. I want to quiet myself to anything except You. Jesus, I am reminded that You call us Your friends and that the things You hear from Your Father You make known to us. O Lord Jesus, help me to live as Your friend always. Amen.

God, Your Word is a lamp unto my feet and a light unto my path. I pray now for the light of Your Word in my life. You long to both meet with me and speak with me, and I pray for that kind of close relationship with You. I boldly come before Your throne of grace, that I would obtain mercy and find grace to help in time of need. Amen.

I pray the same words as Samuel, "Speak Lord, for your servant hears." I pray I would hear nothing except Your voice. I pray that You would confirm to me Your voice by Your Word. Take me to the scripture You want me to read. Bring to mind Your word that You want me to know. Direct my paths and make them straight. Impress upon my heart Your word for my life. Amen.

I pray for the peace of God that rules in my heart—that Your Word and peace would be the deciding factor in how I live. I am reminded in Scripture that You are a good God. Every good gift and every perfect gift is from above, and comes down from the Father of lights, with whom there is no variation or shadow of turning.

I pray now for the strength and power by Your Holy Spirit to obey Your Word. I declare in prayer the words of Scripture that I am God's workmanship, created in Christ Jesus to do good works, which You prepared in advance for me to do. Amen.

I ask all these things now through the Lord Jesus Christ. Amen.

ACKNOWLEDGMENT

I want to thank my good friend and colaborer in the kingdom, Marcus Brotherton. You are gifted by God, a gift from God, and a gift to the body of Christ.

NOTES

Introduction: How Can I Hear God?
1. A. W. Tozer, *Pursuit of God* (Harrisburg, PA: Christian Publications, 1948), 100.

Chapter One: The Beauty of Being Sheep
1. Dallas Willard, *Hearing God* (Downers Grove, IL: IVP Books, 2012), 76–78.

Chapter Two: Why Hear from God?
1. Dallas Willard, *Hearing God* (Downers Grove, IL: IVP Books, 2012), 60.

Chapter Four: Hear God's Voice Through Worship
1. James Strong, *Enhanced Strong's Lexicon* (1995): 4137, from 4134.

Chapter Six: Call for Confirmation
1. I am indebted to missionary Jean Darnall for her teaching on this topic.
2. James Strong, *Enhanced Strong's Lexicon* (1995): 1017 and 1018.

Chapter Seven: Be a Steward of God's Voice
1. Proverbs 1:5, 11:14, 12:15, 24:6.
2. 1 Samuel 8:10; 1 Kings 22:19; 1 Corinthians 14:3; 1 Timothy 4:14.
3. Genesis 31:11, 37:5; 1 Kings 3:5; Acts 16:9, 10:17; Revelation 1:10.
4. James Strong, *Enhanced Strong's Lexicon* (1995): 498, from 473 and the middle voice of 5021.
5. Kirk Dearman, "We Bring the Sacrifice of Praise," John T. Benson Publishing Co., 1984.
6. James Strong, *Enhanced Strong's Lexicon* (1995): 3107, a prolonged form of the poetical *makar* (meaning [is] the same).

Chapter Eight: Recognize God's Voice Through Relationship

1. Watty Piper, *The Little Engine That Could*, original classic ed. (New York: Grosset & Dunlap, 1976).
2. I'm grateful for John Eldredge's thinking on this subject. See his book *Fathered by God* (Nashville, TN: Thomas Nelson, 2009), 32–34.
3. Robert Cottrill, "Today in 1846—William Featherstone Born," *Wordwise Hymns*, July 23, 2010, http://wordwisehymns.com/2010/07/23/today-in-1846-william-ralph-featherstone-born/; see also Tim Challies, "Hymn Stories: My Jesus I Love Thee," *Challies.com*, March 10, 2013, http://www.challies.com/articles/hymn-stories-my-jesus-i-love-thee.

Chapter Nine: Hear God's Voice for Others

1. Matthew 24:36, 50; Matthew 25:13; Mark 13:32.
2. John Davis, *Davis Dictionary of the Bible*, rev. ed. (Nashville, TN: Royal Publishers, Inc., 1973), 658.
3. Johannes P. Louw and Eugene Nida, *Greek-English Lexicon of the New Testament Based on Semantic Domains*, 2nd ed., vol. 1 (New York: United Bible Societies, 1996), 542: 53.79.
4. Alec Rowlands, *The Presence: Experiencing More of God* (Grand Rapids, MI: Tyndale Momentum, 2014), 155–6.

Chapter Ten: Hear God's Voice for a Breakthrough

1. For a fuller treatment on the subject of spiritual warfare, see my book *Truly Free* (Nashville, TN: Thomas Nelson, 2015).
2. James Strong, *Enhanced Strong's Lexicon* (1995): 6010, from 6009; and Francis Brown, S. R. Driver, and Charles A. Briggs, *Enhanced Brown-Driver-Briggs Hebrew and English Lexicon* (Oxford: Clarendon Press, 1977), 952.
3. James Strong, *Enhanced Strong's Lexicon* (1995): 1188, from 1167 and the plural of 6556.

ABOUT THE AUTHOR

Robert Morris is the founding senior pastor of Gateway Church, a multicampus church in the Dallas–Fort Worth Metroplex. Since it began in 2000, the church has grown to more than thirty-six thousand active members.

Robert is featured on the weekly television program *The Blessed Life* and serves as chairman of the board of The King's University. He is the bestselling author of thirteen books, including *The Blessed Life*, *From Dream to Destiny*, *The Power of Your Words*, *The God I Never Knew*, and *Truly Free*.

Robert and his wife, Debbie, have been married thirty-six years and are blessed with one married daughter, two married sons, and six grandchildren. You can follow Robert on Twitter @PsRobertMorris.

The Bible is clear that some problems are actually just problems, but there are other trials you go through that are the work of the enemy in your life. So how can you tell the difference between evil and worldly issues? *Truly Free* will show you the warning signs that your life may be opened to evil and how you can overcome the enemy and find freedom.

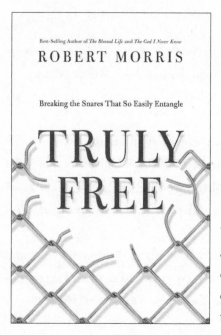

Available in print
and e-book

With relevant scriptures, prayers, and questions for contemplation or group discussion, this book explains how you can find lasting freedom and live *truly free*.

What People Are Saying About *Truly Free*

"*Truly Free* is a great reminder that there is a spiritual battle raging all around us, but we have the victory in Christ. . . . no matter what struggles [we] are facing."

—Joyce Meyer, Bible teacher and bestselling author

"*Truly Free* is a patient unfolding of biblical studies that reveal the Savior's kingdom's power over all that is demonic, deceiving, or destructive of human wholeness."

—Pastor Jack W. Hayford

"Robert Morris reveals the nature of the struggle we all face and the sure ways to win. Every believer needs to read this book."

—Pat Boone, Christian activist and entertainer

BREAK FREE!

IN THIS SIX-SESSION VIDEO-BASED STUDY, BESTSELLING author Robert Morris invites us into this glorious truth: the promise of being set free from sin is a promise to be set free completely. Although evil is real and Christians can be oppressed by it, we have the promise that the One who is in us is greater than the one who is in the world (1 John 4:4). Jesus saves us, trains us to resist the power of evil, and delivers us from anything that holds us back. With Jesus, we can be truly free forever.

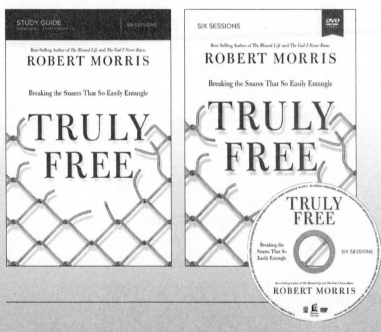

W PUBLISHING GROUP

AN IMPRINT OF THOMAS NELSON

FOR VIDEOS, SAMPLE CHAPTERS, AND OTHER *TRULY FREE* RESOURCES, VISIT TRULYFREEBOOK.COM